Phil 1:3

CHAMPIONS *for* LIFE

CHAMPIONS for LIFE

The Power of a Father's Blessing

BILL GLASS
WITH TERRY PLUTO

Faith Communications
A Division of Health Communications, Inc.

Health Communications, Inc.
Deerfield Beach, Florida

www.hci-online.com

Library of Congress Cataloging-in-Publication Data

Glass, Bill.
Champions for life : the power of a father's blessing / Bill Glass with Terry Pluto.
  p. cm.
  ISBN 0-7573-0250-5
  1. Fathers and sons—Religious aspects—Christianity. 2. Blessing and cursing. I. Pluto, Terry, 1955- II. Title.

BV4529.17.G58 2005
248.8'421—dc22

                                                              2005046038
©2005 Bill Glass
ISBN 0-7573-0250-5

Faith Communications (FC), its Logos and Marks are trademarks of Health Communications, Inc.

Publisher: An Imprint of Health Communications, Inc.
          3201 S.W. 15th Street
          Deerfield Beach, FL 33442-8190

Cover photo ©Imagesource
Cover and inside book design by Lawna Patterson Oldfield

To Mindy, Billy and Bobby,
My children, you have been so easy to bless!
And you've returned that blessing!

—Bill Glass

To Bob Fick,
My spiritual father.

—Terry Pluto

CONTENTS

INTRODUCTION

It's because of a bar of soap."

Those were the first words I ever heard from a prisoner. His name was Roger and he was at Cook County Jail in Chicago.

"Man, they said it was dope," he said. "Ain't no dope, was a bar of soap, you know what I'm sayin'?"

I wasn't sure.

"Since when is it a crime to have a bar a soap?" he asked. "I mean, I didn't do it. Soap is soap, know what I'm sayin'?"

I began to know. He was in jail on drug charges. He said it was soap. The police had another opinion. He ended virtually every sentence with the question, "Know what I'm sayin'?"

I had no clue. Not just about what he was saying, but no idea what I was even doing talking to this poor guy. It was September 1997. I was at Cook County to do a story on Bill Glass and his Champions for Life Ministry for the *Akron Beacon Journal*. Because Bill Glass had been an outstanding defensive end with the Cleveland Browns in the 1960s and because he had this ministry involved with prisons, it sounded like a good story. We're talking about a former all-pro defensive end who has spent the last thirty-four years in prison ministry, speaking in four hundred different institutions each year.

I thought of how it would have been easy for Bill to go the TV evangelist route, a former National Football League (NFL) star doing rallies in stadiums and other high-profile areas. Instead, this was an under the radar "down and dirty ministry," as he calls it. And he touches the lives of the more than 100,000 prisoners who hear him each year.

I figured I'd spend the day with Bill collecting material for a story, just one of 250 stories I write for the paper each year. I watched Bill and Chicago Bears Hall of Famer Mike Singletary talk to several groups of inmates. Both men spoke powerfully about their relationships with their fathers, preaching the likes of which I'd never heard before—and I was astonished how most of the prisoners seemed touched by what they were hearing.

I mentioned this to Bill.

"Most of these guys are hurting, and they really are hungry for the Word of the Lord," he said.

He meant "The Blessing" speech, which has been the heart of his ministry for about thirty years. It's about how we need to feel and hear the unconditional love of a parent, especially a father. And how even aging adults long to be blessed, and how we all ache to know that someone loves us—no matter what. The love of God. The love of a parent. The love that comes with no strings attached, no buts or ifs, just someone saying, "God loves you, and so do I." Listening to Bill, I realized that while I had a very good, hardworking father, he never gave me his full blessing until the very end of his life after he had suffered a stroke. My mother was my biggest fan, the one who found it natural to express unconditional love.

"That's often the case," Glass said. "Mothers are usually better at blessing than fathers; that's why I talk about this so much. Everyone needs to hear this, but especially the fathers."

He talked about finding a spiritual father if your biological father can't or won't bless you. He talked about the power of words to change a life. He talked about how many of us may think we don't need a blessing, but we do. If we looked deep enough and were willing to dig into some areas where we had old wounds, we'd see we needed the healing of a father's blessing. Bill Glass will tell anyone exactly how to do it.

Then Bill suggested that I mingle with the other Teammates (volunteer counselors) in the yard, listen as they talked to the inmates—and maybe visit with a prisoner myself.

"It will give you a better feel for what we do when you write your story," Bill said.

At this point, I was a very new Christian. I had never been to a prison before and had no idea what I was supposed to say to these men. And there was a sea of men, seemingly thousands of them in tan jumpsuits with the letters DOC on their backs— Department of Corrections, as I learned later.

I plunged into this ocean of men and spotted a young, rather chubby (and most of all, safe-looking) man standing in a corner of the yard, away from everyone else.

That was Roger with the soap story.

I'd like to say that the Holy Spirit came down upon Roger and me as we talked in the prison yard that day. I'd like to say that we went over the *Four Spiritual Laws* before he dropped to his knees, tears in his eyes, and asked the Lord for forgiveness. I wish I could say I led him to the nearest sink and baptized him on the spot. But my new friend Roger wasn't much interested in the *Four Laws*, nor was I very adept at explaining them to him, much less giving the Lord a chance to work in his life.

Next, I spotted a tall, thin, thirty-ish black man sucking on a cigarette whose name was Roscoe.

"I first went to jail at fourteen," he said. "Juvy home. Spent four months there. I could have got out earlier, but my mother said she couldn't handle me."

Roscoe hated his father, wherever he happened to be. He wasn't thrilled with his mother either. But now he was a father himself. He had two children—one was nine years old, the other fifteen months. He was doing time on drug charges.

"I was stupid," he said. "I really didn't do what they said."

"Who?" I asked.

"The cops," he said. "But you know, I got a problem."

He paused; I waited. I remembered Bill saying, "You have two ears and one mouth, and God gave it to you that way for a reason. Listen twice as much as you talk."

Finally, Roscoe said, "I'll be clean for a while, have a job and everything . . ."

Then back to drugs.

Then back to jail.

"My wife, she said she wanted to stay with this other guy while I'm here," he said. "I said it was okay. But that didn't work out for her. I mean, I guess she's back with me, but I'm back in here. But I worry about the kids, you know?"

I thought I knew, but I was wrong.

"She's the problem, too," he said.

"Drugs?" I asked.

He nodded.

"I listened to Mr. Glass talk," he said. "I want to be a good father. I want my kids to, you know, look up to me. But I'm in here . . ."

His voice trailed off.

"Being in a place like this, it makes you think," he said.

I knew exactly what Roscoe was saying, because being in Cook County Jail was having a profound impact on me, far beyond the scope of my story. I watched and listened as the Teammates talked to the inmates. Men with sunken, bloodshot, hopeless eyes and hunched shoulders. Or men with huge muscles, angry tattoos and scars on their faces. Or a few men who looked like someone who could have lived next door to me.

Lost souls.

Those words came to my mind, although I wasn't much better if I was being utterly honest with myself. But that thought wouldn't come to me until long after I left Cook County. It would come one night when I couldn't sleep and I stared at the ceiling, still seeing the faces of some of the men I'd met that day in jail.

I saw some of myself in them, but that came later.

But what I immediately saw that day in the prison yard was real down-in-the-trenches Christianity. I had worked in an urban soup kitchen. I had tutored inner-city kids. But I was forty-one years old and I'd never tried to lead anyone to the Lord. I had no idea how to do it and thought it was a job meant for someone else. But that day in Cook County, I saw a couple old men in wheelchairs talking to inmates so tough they could reduce a block of concrete to dust with just their steely eyes. These men were listening to those older Teammates in the wheelchairs.

Then I saw other inmates sitting on the grass, talking to a nondescript, middle-aged insurance salesman. It was impossible to imagine these men saying three words to each other because they seemed to have so little in common, but after a while, they joined hands and prayed.

None of this was happening with television coverage. None of this was designed to raise money or stroke anyone's ego. It was pure evangelism, the likes of which I never even knew existed, much less could be available to someone like me.

I said to myself, "So this is what real Christians do."

I had first talked to Bill Glass in 1996 when I was writing a book called *Browns Town, 1964*. It was about the 1964 Browns, the last Cleveland team to win an NFL Championship. I tracked down all the key players from that team and did a "Where are

They Now?" section at the end of the book. That was when I first heard about Bill and his prison ministry.

At that point in my life, I was a token member of a large denomination. I had mastered the art of coming to the service late, leaving a little early and thinking that was a relationship with God. While writing that *Browns'* book, Bill and I spoke several times on the phone as he graciously shared football and prison stories for my book. He sent me material about his ministry. I thought it was interesting, but the last thing I wanted was to go to jail—for any reason. What would I ever have to say to those guys? Why would they listen to me? Besides, I was in favor of throwing away the key and letting them all burn in their self-made hell.

Very Christian, don't you think?

That was 1996, and I didn't think much about it for a year.

In September 1997, the *Browns Town, 1964* book was published, and some fans said they enjoyed the section about Bill Glass working in the prisons. I thought it would make a good story for the Akron *Beacon Journal.* It became a good story, but it was far more than that. That day at Cook County Jail changed my life. It made me realize that I didn't know God, and it inspired me to sincerely reach out to him for the first time in my life. I began to read the Bible, something I hadn't done since grade school. At this point all I knew about Jesus Christ was that I didn't know him or what he wanted from me. But I did know that all my achievements in journalism and as an author meant very little to me at the age of forty-one.

Bill Glass had said something that struck me: "We spend the first forty years of our life looking for success and the next forty seeking significance."

What began as nothing more than another story to me became a life-changing ministry. After a while, I felt my faith growing enough that I thought I could at least try to be a "real Christian" and enlisted as one of Bill's foot soldiers for Champions for Life. I went to one prison in Georgia, another in Oregon and another in North Carolina. I just kept wanting to go back and talk about the Lord. I found I needed it as much (or maybe more) than the inmates. I began to volunteer at my local jail, where I've been leading weekly Bible classes and services for more than six years. Bill's ministry and blessing message changed my life. It also helped my marriage, as I began to bless my wife regularly—to keep encouraging her, to praise her daily and to do it from the heart.

This is my twenty-second published book, and it means as much to me as any of the first twenty-one. It's a book that I know will change lives because Bill's blessing message changed mine.

I believe that the Lord led me to this project, starting with my call to Bill for my book on the Cleveland Browns. That should have been the beginning and end of our relationship, but something about Bill's prison ministry stayed with me, sort of like a piece of gum on the bottom of my shoe. No matter what I did, it stuck to me. The turning point was the last inmate I met on that first day in Cook County Jail. His name was Jackson and he was scared. He was eighteen years old, but looked like a skinny fifteen-year-old, and he was to be released in a few days.

"I don't want to get into all of what happened," he said. "But I was on house arrest, then I broke it to go talk to the mailman."

Great, another ridiculous story, I thought.

Then Jackson said he heard Bill talk about being a father. He said he didn't have any children, but he wanted to be a father, a good father. A better father than the man who disappeared from his life.

"I've been thinking about God and stuff," he said.

So we talked about fathers and sons and God.

"Will you pray with me?" he asked. "I don't do it so good."

"Neither do I," I said.

But I reached out and took his hands. We closed our eyes, and together we prayed. As I walked out of Cook County Jail, I thought about what had just happened with Jackson. I realized that was the essence of prison ministry—two guys who had never met before reaching out and praying together. One older white man—me—blessing a younger black man.

I thought about Bill's blessing message, how it is so simple yet so powerful because it's so true. All of us are hurting. All of us need to know that God loves us. All of us need the healing touch of a father's hand—a heavenly *and* an earthly father. All of us need a spiritual father if our biological father is not there for us. All of us need to tell others they are loved—unconditionally. All of us need to be blessed, and all of us are called to bless others.

That's where God's healing begins. I knew it then, that Bill's message was something everyone needed to hear. That is the message Bill delivers as he shares his stories in this book.

—Terry Pluto

ACKNOWLEDGMENTS

The authors have so many people to thank. At the head of the list are Pat Fulkerson and Kim Huff, who served as the administrative assistants to Bill Glass and are the spiritual mothers to this book. Their patience and caring is the reason there is a book. Amy Hughes did an outstanding job as editor, with great backing from copy editor Cathy Slovensky. The book was originally the idea of Pat Williams, and agent Faith Hamlin helped bring the project along. The authors would also like to thank Eddie Siebert, Steve Haley, Bishop Joey Johnson and especially our wives—Mavis Glass and Roberta Pluto.

—*Bill Glass and Terry Pluto*

Chapter One

CATCHING A FATHER'S BLESSING . . .

I remember playing catch with my father.

There is something special about a father playing catch with a child. Or putting that child up on his shoulders, making her feel like she's on top of the world. Or simply holding her hand, her feeling so small but so safe in the hands of a father who loves her.

That's part of the blessing, the touch. And we all need a blessing.

My father knew this. He was a big, strong man. Most of us who had good fathers remember them as big, strong men—at least when seeing them through the eyes of a child. I couldn't imagine anyone throwing a baseball harder than my father did when we played catch on our immaculate lawn. My mitt would POP and my hand would ache as I caught what I thought was his best fastball. Best of all, my confidence would soar. My father's name was Vernon Glass, and he was a good pitcher, a real pitcher. He had played professionally in the Class AA Texas League. He was a left-hander with a fastball that whistled through the air, and the batters heard the *whoosh*. Our family lore was that my father quit minor league baseball so he could get a job that paid better and raise a family. We believe he would have made the major leagues if he had stuck with it, but who knows?

The point is my father was a professional pitcher, and he was playing catch with me. He probably wasn't using anything close to his best stuff, but that didn't matter. He threw. His ball was a white *blur*, a *whoosh* and a *slap* against my leather glove. And I caught it.

When our game of catch was over, he'd put his arm around me and we'd walk into the house together, both smiling. He was my father and I knew he loved me, no matter what.

This is what we all want, a parent's blessing.

My father knew this. Most nights, he'd come to my bed. He'd rub my back or at least run his giant hand through my hair. He'd always say that he was proud of me, that I was a fine boy. Then he'd kiss me. This enormous, physical man was the epitome of masculinity. But he was smart enough and loving enough to know his son needed to be hugged, kissed and told he was wonderful. Not just once, but every night. No matter if the day had been good or bad for us, his last words were those of affirmation and love. I remember him spanking me only once. My older brother was an all-state quarterback in high school. I loved his all-star jacket, and I knew that I wasn't supposed to wear it. I was *told* by Dad to not even *think* about putting it on. The jacket belonged to my brother. One day, I took it to school and wore it proudly. When my father came home from work, he took off his belt and whacked me. I'm sure it was not very hard, and only a few times. But it did sting. My father had an Irish temper. His face would turn scarlet, his neck would bulge and you were sure he was about to burst a blood vessel. For a few minutes, he'd yell and rant and carry on . . . and a few minutes later, he'd come back and apologize. He knew he had a bad temper and hated it when he lost control.

We knew about the temper, too.

That's why he could keep my brother, my sister and me in line with just his *stare*. He could stop a roaring freight train with one hard, Vernon Glass glance. It hurt worse than any spanking because we knew it meant we had disappointed him, and we hated to let down the man who loved us so much. His stare was more frightening than any scream. His stare was also a way to say that he cared about us, about what we were doing, and about teaching us the right way to grow up. But every night, that stare was gone when he came into our bedroom. This was when he reminded us that we mattered to him. This also was a way of making us know that we mattered to God, a God who loved us like our father. I wouldn't realize that until much later, but my father's love made it easier for me to love God . . . trust in God . . . have a relationship with God. Too many men won't do this with their children, especially their sons. They're almost afraid to tell their children, especially the sons, that they are loved. In some cases, their own fathers didn't deliver that crucial message. Or they may fear they'll be seen as soft and unmanly if they treated their own children with that kind of love. My father was a professional athlete, and later a hard-driving businessman, but his heart was big enough to bless us. He spoke to our hearts with words of love, words of acceptance. He used words that made a difference in my life. Since then, I've learned that so many people have never heard these healing words.

I played in the NFL for eleven years with the Cleveland Browns and Detroit Lions. I was a member of four Pro Bowl teams. I was a defensive end, where I fought with huge linemen so I could get to the guy with the ball and throw him to the turf. I'm blessed to hold the Cleveland Browns record for quarterback sacks in a season. There were some games that were nothing more than brawls, hand-to-hand combat. I'm not talking about dirty play, but hard, physical, demanding—and yes, manly—battles. But I've learned from my own father that I need to be tender and loving with my children, and I'm not afraid to show it. Nor do I care who knows it. That's because we all need a blessing.

You may not have had a parent who blessed you, a parent who said, "No matter what, I'll always love you."

Maybe you didn't have a father who protected you, or a father who thought you were special and told you so. You may think, "I didn't have that, but I turned out all right."

Don't bet on it. Take a moment, search deep inside for a little hole in your heart that still needs to be filled. Don't deny the pain. The only way to heal is to first admit you are hurting. Unless you had a father bless you—or someone who stepped in and became your spiritual father—you have an ache in your soul, a hole in your heart. If you're completely honest with yourself, you know this is true. You know it during those nights you stare at the ceiling and wonder if anyone will ever love and believe in you. Those nights when you're so exhausted, yet can't sleep. Those nights when you know something is wrong, but you're not sure what.

It's the longing for the approval of the Father, both on earth and heaven.

Words matter.

Words can bless or bleed.

Words spoken are very hard to take back.

I've heard parents say almost flippantly, "You're stupid."

Or, "Don't be so dumb."

Or, "You're so irritating."

Some parents believe these words will make the child shape up and fly right. It's like a challenge, the parent saying, "Prove me wrong." All they do is injure the self-image of the child. What a dad whispers in a child's ear sounds like a scream, and the message can heal or wound. A parent's voice is a megaphone straight to the heart of the child.

My own son, Bobby, said to me, "Remember when you yelled at me?"

I don't remember it that way. I know I didn't yell, I only said something very quietly and calmly—yet in his mind, that was screaming in his ear. I was always very careful never to make negative statements to my children. Even since they've been adults, I've noticed they are very anxious to hear only positive words from me. So I've made an art form of saying things that lift them up, not tear them down. They are now in middle age, and they still want—and need—a blessing from their father. Even now that I have to physically look up to my own sons. Words we heard as children can haunt us into adulthood. Words that blessed us as children can accompany us into old age, long after the person who spoke them into our lives has died. The book of John opens by telling us, "In the beginning was the Word." God spoke the world into being. Creation was accomplished through the spoken word of God. And we can speak life into the souls and hearts of our children.

Words are how we are to begin blessing our children, as my own father demonstrated. He died at the age of forty-five. I was fourteen. I still remember his presence, his words, his touch, his blessing.

Jim Sundberg heard me talking like this one day in a chapel service when he was playing for the Texas Rangers. He was their star catcher, and he came up to me after my message and said, "What you say is true, Bill, because I remember when I was a little boy my daddy would say, 'You're going to be a great major-league catcher.' And I said, 'But Dad, I threw the ball over the second baseman's head.' My dad said, 'Yes, you've got a terrific arm.' And I'd say, 'But Dad, I struck out,' and he'd say, 'What a swing—what a swing.' No matter what I did, he turned it to reinforce his dream, and it became my dream as well."

Parents can inspire or destroy dreams in a single sentence. Children don't need parents to act like coaches, because coaches usually praise, then withhold the blessing. They do this to squeeze just a little more out of the athlete. This might work in sports, but not at home. Children need a parent, especially a father, who speaks the words of love, hope and belonging into their lives. Even if you don't know how, or if this sounds strange to you, your children need it. And you can do it.

In fact, you must do it!

The future of your children, and your children's children, and even their children depends upon it.

Numbers 14:18 reads: "God does not leave the guilty unpunished, he punishes the children for the sin of the fathers to the third and fourth generations."

What happens to our children? Our children's children? Their children and the generations to follow? It can begin with us.

How do we do that?

Consider this from Deuteronomy 7:9: "The Lord your God is God. He is the faithful God keeping his covenant of love to a thousand generations for those who love him and keep his commandments."

How do we do that?

We love and bless our children.

PERSONAL APPLICATION AND PRAYER

✝ Two of the most memorable of my father's blessings were a game of catch and his nightly bedside ritual. Both included at least one, if not all three, of these demonstrations of blessing—hugs, kisses and positive words.

✝ Real men aren't afraid of warmth and tenderness.

✝ Our relationship to our earthly father impacts our relationship to God. It's tough to love your Heavenly Father if you hate your earthly father.

✝ These warm, positive words and hugs are formative and pivotal to our children and their children— for generations.

Prayer

Oh God, please don't allow me to fail
at this most pivotal point. Give me the guts
to speak words and give hugs and kisses of blessing
into the lives of my children and grandchildren
so that it echoes for generations to come.
May my blessing to them point them toward you,
the ultimate Father. In the name of
Jesus Christ our Lord, Amen.

Chapter Two

THE CURSE

I had a face-lift.

I am a former defensive end and I look like it. I'm big. I'm battle-scarred, and I'm not a guy who spends a lot of time worrying about what I wear. But my wrinkles have always bothered me. I felt ugly and insecure.

One day I had a face-lift.

It pains me to say that, even though it happened twenty-five years ago. It has to do with a part of me that was five years old when I heard my mother talking to a friend. They were in another room, and they had no idea that I was listening.

"I love William dearly," my mother said. "But he's not that good-looking."

She almost whispered it, but a curse doesn't need to be a scream.

My own sweet mother was saying I was ugly! At least, that was the way I heard it. Until that point, I hadn't thought much about my appearance. I was only five, and I had received nothing but unconditional love at home. I knew my mother loved me, but she said I wasn't good-looking. My mother was a great mother. I still love her. It would break her heart to know that I heard what she said. I wouldn't be talking about it if she were still alive because I wouldn't want to hurt her feelings. But I must admit her words stayed with me for the rest of my life. It was like a voodoo curse, a nail driven into my heart. I would never want to say anything to hurt her. But since she is with the Lord, I think I can use this example to help others and prove a point: We can hurt those we truly love with our words.

How so?

Ever watch a young woman try on a new dress and show it to Mom—and especially Dad—and then burst into tears when the parent didn't bless her choice of the dress? When Mom said, "Oh, honey, you're not really going to wear that, are you?" Or Dad said, "I guess it's OK."

Words mean so much to us.

And I couldn't get it out of my head that my own mother thought I was ugly. It hurt. I know men aren't supposed to admit that. We're not supposed to care what people say about us. My goal in life was never to win a beauty contest, but we want the approval of those who mean the most to us, especially our parents. When I was a teenager and my face was ravaged with acne, I didn't see myself as just another teenager with a bad case of pimples. I was very self-conscious. Every mirror I've peered into through the years reinforced my mother's evaluation of my looks. Even when my wife and friends assure me that I'm not "that ugly" I don't believe them. My jobs have had absolutely nothing to do with my looks, yet I still worry about my looks. I know I am beautiful in the eyes of God. But it still bothers me that my face looks like a beat-up Dodge after a demolition derby, with fenders dragging on the ground, doors dented, glass broken, the roof ripped off.

I've never talked about the face-lift before. I'm mentioning it now to make a point: *Words matter.* Plastic surgeons have discovered that no matter how drastically they change the appearance, the patient tends to see only their poor self-image in the mirror. Our society continually tells us that we're too fat, too skinny, too old, too thin, too *something.* Oh, we also have bad breath and lousy hair. Just watch the commercials on TV if you want to get an immediate inferiority complex. It's why most women think there is something wrong with their bodies, even famous supermodels. Somebody said something to make them think so. It could have been a relative, or it could have been the unrealistic standards set by Hollywood and Madison Avenue as they try to sell the ideal vision of how a woman should look.

Fortunately, the blessings from my father and mother were more potent than one careless remark from my mother. I was also blessed with lots of positive reinforcement and encouragement in other important areas—athletics, ministry and finding my own masculinity, thanks to excellent role models. But my mother's curse is unbroken. I still believe I'm ugly! I pack on too much weight. I mean, I'm fat and I know it. I don't dress neatly. I don't care about my appearance enough because my natural tendency is to "live up" to or "down to" my mother's assessment. I have tried crash diets, aerobic exercise, weight lifting and swimming. I can't even remember all the diets and programs that I've attempted, other than to know that none of them worked for very long. I still feel the frustration and sense of failure. Right now, I'm on a form of the Atkins diet and I walk at least thirty minutes each day. I want to lose weight. I want to be healthy. I want to look better. But most of the time, I just look and feel like I've always looked and felt.

That can be discouraging.

After enduring the pain and expense of surgery, I looked into the mirror certain I'd find a new handsome face staring back at me.

Instead, I saw . . . me!

It wasn't that the doctor had failed. What I saw in the mirror wasn't a true reflection. It was my own self-image. No matter what the surgeon could have done, all I saw were my flaws. I paid a high price to learn that obvious truth. It wasn't so much *how* I looked, but how I *thought* I looked. My self-image was based on my mother's words when I was five years old!

My mother never intended to hurt me, much less curse me. It's a wound, and big guys have wounds, too. That includes those of us who played against Vince Lombardi's Green Bay Packers in zero-degree temperatures. The pain from that curse in my life was worse than any hit I ever took on the field. That's because I knew football was a violent game, and I expected the physical punishment and mental anguish that came when someone ran right over me for a touchdown. I could handle cleat marks all over my body. I could deal with the physical pain. But the mental war can sometimes seem like a losing battle.

Several years ago, I was checking into a hotel room in Los Angeles.

"You look just like a movie star," said the clerk.

That was the first time anyone had ever said that to me. A movie star?

"Really!" I said. "Which star?"

"I can't remember his name," she said.

We continued to talk about my room, and as I finished filling out the paperwork she said, "Now I remember."

"Who?" I asked.

"Herman Munster," she said.

I had to laugh to keep from crying. I was hoping it might be someone like Harrison Ford; instead it's a guy who looked like Frankenstein. From a stranger, it's annoying but easier to handle. But at home, everyone wants that unconditional love from a parent. Over the years, I've told myself that how I looked didn't matter. Besides, I can't change it, so I might as well learn to live with it.

The truth is most people don't care. Few notice my own curse because they are fighting their own. Here are some examples:

You're stupid.

Or skinny.

Or fat.

Or ugly.

Or just like your father, who was a drunk.

Or like your brother, who's in prison.

Or you just won't amount to much.

These things shouldn't matter, but they often do, especially if we hear them early and often in life. They can stick with you like a glob of gum on the bottom of your shoe. Ever notice how hard it is to get rid of all of it? You try to pull it off, and the gum clings to your fingers. It expands like a rubber band. You pull your hand away, and you still have some gum on your fingers and some more on the bottom of your shoe. It's everywhere else—often on your clothes, even in your hair! Maybe the best thing to do is just throw away the shoes and buy a new pair.

But it's hard to do that with your parents' words and actions. You're stuck with them; they're stuck to you. Sometimes their words are like glue, holding you back from the person God wants you to become. Psalm 139:13–14 says, "For you created my innermost being, you knit me together in my mother's womb. I praise you because I am fearfully and wonderfully made."

The Psalms are nothing more than prayers that someone—usually David—simply wrote to God. David would say, "God don't make junk." And God doesn't. Parents need to remember that. The child must hear words that bless from the moment of birth, if not sooner. That's right, you can bless in the womb. Blessing should start in the fetal stages and continue until death. I blessed all of my children by placing my hands on their mother's pregnant womb and praying. I learned this from my father. He died when my sister Linda was only two years old. She has no conscious memory of him, but she is so much like him that it must be more than genetic. He adored her—his only daughter. He loved and hugged and kissed her constantly! Some of the best surviving pictures of him are flickering pictures from early home movies now over fifty years old. He is playing with her in the grass of our backyard, sitting with her on her level on the lawn—then on all fours—smiling in love for her even though the ravages of Hodgkin's disease are obvious in his thin body and face. Some of his last words were for her protection—"Where's Linda? Don't let her get out in the street. Let me see Linda. Bring her to me. I must see her one last time." His adoration carried a blessing, which seeped into her subconscious. When a parent genuinely blesses, it carries through into future generations, even transcending conscious awareness. While Linda lived in the same house and was extremely close to her mother for more than fifty years, she's actually more like her dad. It's amazing how profoundly her father impacted her through that blessing and in the first two years of her life, even though she can't consciously remember anything about him.

Too often parents try to teach humility. I say teach confidence—that God didn't make a mistake when your child was born. People who have been cursed the worst often end up in prison. Or they bounce from job to job, from relationship to relationship, from religion to religion. Some of them also brag the most, as if compensating for the blessing they never received at home. If no one will bless and value them, they'll do it themselves. The inmate who brags about his toughness, his smarts, his muscles, his crimes or his sexual exploits is usually applying his own form of verbal deodorant to a stinking self-image. I've often asked a group of inmates, "How many of you had mothers or fathers who said that you'd end up in jail one day?"

Most of the hands are raised. The parents' prophecy had become reality.

Several years ago I was walking down death row in Parchman, Mississippi. Forty-four men were on death row at the time, and I asked every man the same question, "How do you and your dad get along?"

Forty-four out of forty-four men said they had a poor relationship with their fathers. Either they had active hatred or complete indifference for their fathers. There wasn't one man on death row who even hinted that he respected and loved his father. In several prisons, they make cards available for inmates to mail to their mothers on Mother's Day. Usually, the cards are immediately claimed, written and mailed. When it comes time for Father's Day, most of the cards sit in the box. Inmates know no one in their lives worthy of the title "father." Prison is a wasteland, a place where you are sent because they don't think you belong with the "good" people outside. It's a negative environment where most conversations are put-downs and insults.

One inmate told me, "My earliest memories are of my parents not wanting me. They sent me to live with my grandparents. They didn't want me, either. I felt rejected. When I tried to play with other kids, they usually didn't let me into their games. At school, I didn't seem to fit. I didn't think my teachers liked me. It seems girls didn't like me. The athletes rejected me, and so did the hell-raisers. In my late teens, I robbed a liquor store and was thrown into prison. For the first time in my life, I felt accepted because I was with a bunch of other rejects."

That's the kind of story that you hear over and over when you get inmates alone and they begin to open their hearts. These testimonials serve as warnings and help us to understand them a little more, and understand how to keep our children from ending up in the same situations. Everyone longs for a blessing; few receive it. The consequences of not experiencing the blessing can be serious. The FBI conducted a study on seventeen young men who shot their classmates in schools. These were not inner-city drive-by shootings; these were shootings in towns like Paducah, Kentucky; Littleton, Colorado; Pearl, Mississippi—mostly middle-class towns in middle-class neighborhoods. The FBI discovered there was only one common denominator among them: a bad relationship with their fathers. In my own experience, I've found that there's something within that makes a man mean when he doesn't get along with his daddy. Just as it's true that hurt people hurt people. There are a lot of hurting people in the world, and a lot of the wounds were inflicted by parents, especially fathers.

Watch any football game on TV and you'll see a player say, "Hi, Mom!"

You seldom ever see a player say, "Hi, Dad."

Why is that?

Because mothers do a better job of blessing their children.

I remember my mother watching me play football in school. Her eyes were always on me, and her heart was with me. She didn't care about the coaching, the score or anything but her son. I knew it and felt blessed. It seems to me that the hearts of women generally find it easier to bless. One season with the Browns, we had lost a tough road game and our plane arrived late at Cleveland Hopkins Airport. We had won the week before, and a mob of fans greeted us. We knew it would be a different story this time.

As our plane landed, one of the players joked, "I bet there will be a huge crowd just waiting for us."

Lose a game like we did and you don't expect anyone to greet you. It was a snowy night. As we taxied to the terminal, I saw no one on the same observation deck where there were about a thousand fans the week before. Another player said, "Yep, they'll have the brass band out for us, bet they can't wait to welcome the conquering heroes."

That night, there were no TV cameras, no reporters, no one at all outside. It was a complete change from the previous Sunday.

"This town sure loves a winner," said another player.

Of course, we didn't expect anyone to be there because we lost.

But when we entered the terminal, there was a huge sign: WE LOVE YOU, BROWNS!

Our wives had made it. They blessed us. We all need a blessing, especially when we're feeling like we're losing.

A female inmate once told me, "My dad didn't bless me, he beat me."

Another quietly wept about her father sexually exploiting her "since I can remember."

What kind of father would do such a thing as this? Too many! A startling number of women bring men into their homes—some who have served time for sex crimes—and expose her children to these men. When signs of abuse occur, the woman often ignores them. She is more worried about her own need for a man than the risk she's taking with her children. They too often even blame the children for the problem. After a while, the children believe it. They begin to think they are "dirty" and "bad," somehow responsible for the abuse they've received. Long after the physical wounds have scarred over and healed, the heart still bleeds, the soul aches.

Those children grow up longing for a blessing, but never quite believe they're worth it. For women, this often leads to looking for love in all the wrong places and hooking up with all the wrong men. Why do so many women who were physically abused—and whose mothers were physically abused—marry men who beat them? Or girls from alcoholic homes marry men who drink too much?

It's a generational curse.

Fathers, do you want your daughters to marry the right kind of man?

Then bless your daughters. Tell them how they are beautiful to you and to God. Say it over and over again, every day. Give them a feeling of protection and acceptance.

Do you want them to marry a good man who will bless them and treat them right? Then show them what that man looks like by being that man. My home was an affectionate one where my father openly displayed his love for my mother and us. My father always kissed my mother good night, and my parents kissed me good night. My father blessed us with a word and a touch. He did it out loud and with lots of hugs. He did it in front of everyone. He modeled what it means to be a husband and a father.

Remember, daughters often marry men just like their fathers, just as sons often take after their fathers. Not every person who fails to receive a blessing ends up in prison or in a dismal domestic situation, but many people have been cursed by a lack of a blessing. Do you know anyone who is an overachiever? A perfectionist? Someone who is never content, never able to accept a compliment? Ever run into someone whom you tried to praise, but they immediately rejected it—and then told you what was wrong with the thing that had impressed you so much? These people can drive you crazy. They can't even just say, "Thank you!" They are forever competing, always trying to measure up to some standard they will never meet. Often, they didn't receive a blessing, and they are paying for the neglect of their parents. It's a wound that scabs over, but never fully heals.

One day, I was in a restaurant in New Mexico. The waitress told me, "That's such a fine young family."

She was talking about the new doctor who had recently come to town. He was with his very beautiful wife and young boy. They seemed like the perfect family.

Then I heard the father yell, "You dummy!"

His son was ready to burst into tears. His wife was silent, embarrassed. During the conversation, he also called his son "an ignoramus . . . foolish . . . stupid."

What could the boy at dinner have possibly done to deserve that kind of ridicule? I don't even remember him spilling anything. I have a feeling that was how the doctor's father had talked to him, and he was just passing down the curse. Listening to that, I thought, "You may be a great doctor, a real healer, but you are hurting your child for life."

I have a friend whose father called him "Half-a-job."

He never talked about this while his father was alive. Like the situation with my mother, he would not want to say anything to a parent whom he loved while that parent was alive, especially because my friend knows he had a very good father—not perfect, but far better than most. But even good fathers make mistakes. Their stories teach us how we should deal with our children.

My friend is now in his late forties and very successful. But part of him spent far too much time trying to achieve just to prove his father wrong. His father also yelled whenever my friend would spill something. More than forty years later, my friend still almost shakes and wants to hide under the table when he accidentally knocks over a cup of water. Although he knows it's not a big deal, he feels as if he failed his father. Inside, he does cry over spilled milk.

My father was the opposite.

When I spilled something, it upset my mother's sense of order and angered her. My father would just wave it off, telling her not to make such a big deal out of a little mess.

"Hey, he's just a kid, and kids spill things; he didn't do it on purpose," he'd say.

My father blessed me by defending me.

Words have such power . . .

Women usually are far ahead of men in this department, but I've seen some mothers who are just as stuck as some fathers in this area. I heard one mom say, "When you look at me in my grave, you'll wish you'd treated me better."

That's not a blessing, it's a curse. There's never any reason to say something like that to anyone. Or this one: "Every time you do something like that you put another nail in my casket."

What a heavy burden to strap on a child for the rest of his life—he is unlikely to erase it from his mind.

Once a mother introduced me to her children.

"This is my little girl. She is very timid," said the mother.

The girl stood there frightened, her fingers in her mouth.

"This is my little boy," she said. "He's a bully."

He stood there, chest out, muscles flexed and ready for a fight.

"This is my other little boy," she said. "Sometimes he can be kind of dumb."

The boy stood there obviously feeling stupid.

Often, children become what parents say they will become. As parents, we have the power to create a vision in the heads of our children that lives long after Mom and Dad are dead and the children have reached middle age.

I was watching a television interview with Kirk Douglas, who had just written his autobiography, *The Ragman's Son*.

The interviewer asked, "Mr. Douglas, is there anything you regret?"

Kirk said, "I never got the blessing from my ragman father. I never had his approval."

He is one of the greatest movie stars of all times, perhaps one of the most successful men our country has ever produced. All his father did was sell rags on the streets of Philadelphia, but he never gave his son Kirk Douglas a blessing, and Kirk never got over it. He was on national television with tears streaming down his cheeks. His memories were as fresh as yesterday. He never got the approval of the ragman. He titled his book *The Ragman's Son* because he could never escape the curse of his ragman father.

God the Father delivered perhaps the clearest example of a blessing in history. It was at the baptism of his son, Jesus Christ.

"This is my beloved Son in whom I'm well pleased" (Matt. 3:17).

Jesus performed no miracles until he heard his Father's blessing. His ministry that would change the world really began with that blessing on the day of his baptism. It launched him into his ministry, giving him identity and purpose. God did not bless his son because of something he did or said, but rather simply because Jesus *is* his son. That's exactly how we should treat our children. They must know they are "well pleasing" to us because they are our children, not because of something they do. And they must hear these words often, and the words must be spoken out loud and sincerely.

In Deuteronomy 30:19, God says, "I have set before you life and death, blessing and cursing . . . choose life so that you and your children may live."

PERSONAL APPLICATION AND PRAYER

✞ Christ's ministry began at his baptism. *"You are my Son whom I love:" with you I am well pleased.* (Luke 3:22) How important was this blessing? Before it, Christ did little of note. After the blessing, he was so powerful that we divide history by his life: B.C. and A.D.

✞ If blessing made such an earthshaking, historical watershed impact on the life of Christ and the world, then it is of pivotal importance for earthly fathers to do likewise.

✞ My mother's "whispered" curse . . . my face-lift . . . the awesome power of the unguarded curse! A highly negative society reinforced my curse.

✞ My younger sister's blessing impacted her life even though she was so young she has no conscious memory of being blessed by her father.

✞ The curse is always evident on death row.

✞ Women often do a better job of blessing than men. Watch what you say. You may curse them by those offhand curses like, *"Don't be so stupid!" "Dummy!" "You're going to end up in prison."* You intend to warn them against disaster, but your words curse them toward the very thing you are warning them against.

PRAYER

Lord, guide my words that I may bless and not curse those who follow in my lineage.
For Christ's sake, Amen.

Chapter Three

THE BUBBLE OF EMPTINESS

Why don't we want to talk about the blessing?

Because most of us don't want to admit that we weren't blessed by our parents. So we don't want to bless our kids, our spouses or even our friends because we don't know how to do it. Or we don't feel comfortable doing it. Or we just don't get it. Or maybe we don't want to sound like a phony, as some people do when they are encouraging others. We tend to think, "That guy can't be real. He's just running some kind of con game."

Sometimes that's true, but not always.

When I was with the Browns, I got a letter from a kid in New York who said he wanted to start a fan club for me.

"I've followed your career closely," he wrote. "I think you're the greatest football player in the NFL. I watch every move you make when you're on TV. Can you send me an autographed picture?"

Being a lineman, I didn't have a fan club. Nor do linemen receive much attention from fans or the media. So I mailed him the picture. Then I noticed another player on the team got the same letter as I did. As did another player. And another player. It was copied and sent to almost every player on our team—so the kid could get the autographed pictures.

Most blessings aren't a scam. Most blessings are sincere. But much of the time, there is no blessing, and many of us don't even try to bless the people we love. After I recently spoke at a church, I received this e-mail: "Your message really hit home with me. I wanted to come down during the invitation, but I was afraid I'd be a blubbering mess. Growing up, I had a great dad, but he had problems saying 'I love you.' My grandfather was a great man and had a Ph.D in engineering. But he also was lacking in the emotional department. When he was about seventy, I was talking to him on the phone. I had the urge to say, 'I love you,' which was not normal in our family. His reply was, 'Oh, um, OK.' That was kind of funny at the time, but I just wanted him to know. I wish I had told him that more often. It's so true how generations that don't get the blessing find it's so hard to give one."

That's because a blessing doesn't seem to fit into most of our worlds. The places we live are tough, frustrating, overwhelming, angry and too fast-paced. Exposing our feelings means running the risk of rejection, or at least appearing foolish. But Paul was so right when he wrote in 1 Corinthians 4:10: "We are fools for Christ." We have to be willing to seem ridiculous in the eyes of most of the world to bring forth the power of God's blessing in our lives and those we love. Most young fathers are not embarrassed to make gurgling noises and baby talk with their infants— and they don't care who is watching. Why not be willing to bless those same children when they are older and desperate for our approval? Hug them. Encourage them. Tell them they are loved, that you are proud of them and believe in them. Find something you like about them and mention it. Don't dwell on the negative. Don't constantly critique them. Try to remember what it was like to be their age and to feel desperate for approval.

When I played pro football, I felt like I had a foot in two worlds. For six months each year, I hit people, I sacked the quarterback, I played a violent game and I played hard. Not dirty. I wasn't trying to hurt anyone. But I wanted to hit you hard enough to get the job done. If you lined up across from me, you knew you'd get my best shot. There's a difference between hitting hard to win and hitting hard to injure someone—and the players know it. I never crossed that line, which is how a Christian can play football. At the same time I was in the NFL, I spent six years studying for my divinity degree and graduated from seminary in 1963. I played through the 1968 season. I had bones cracked, skin ripped off, been knocked unconscious, torn ligaments and countless other injuries. The point I'm making is to play pro football, you have to be a rugged guy.

You may live in the same type of world. Maybe it's not football, but it's the battle that takes place every day in some businesses. It can be the ultracompetitive world of sales. Maybe it's the area of law, where the warfare is held in a courtroom. Or perhaps it's the fight just to make enough money to pay the bills and not lose your soul in the process. You still compete. Some days you feel beat up, if not physically, then mentally. You are tired. You work for a boss who sees you as nothing more than a machine that happens to be powered by blood and a heart instead of a power line and electricity. You may have been fired or downsized. You may have had to take a cut in pay or benefits. You probably have had a point in your life when things just weren't fair.

This can make anyone a little hard-hearted. It can make you think the world is a tough place where you need to be strong just to grind out a living. You want to prepare your children for what they will be facing. You don't want them to wilt the first time the heat of life hits them. The temptation is to be overly critical, to push them, to be so concerned with spoiling them that you fail to nurture and encourage them.

Somewhere in this battle, the blessing is lost.

Well, I bless my kids, and I know it doesn't make them soft.

It strengthens them for the challenges they will face in life. I've talked to some of the biggest, strongest, toughest guys you can imagine. They are not afraid of anything, or at least you'd think that. But they've told me, "I'll be a leader in the church. I'll read my Bible. I'll pray during my quiet time. I'll give money. But don't ask me to pray out loud over my kids. Don't ask me to share my faith with anyone. Don't expect me to do this blessing thing."

I call these guys "Gutless wonders."

I wonder how they can be so heartless to hold back something their kids need desperately. I wonder why they are so afraid of being the spiritual leader of the family. I wonder why some of these men could play in the NFL like me, line up across from a guy who looks like he ate raw meat and rusty railroad spikes for breakfast, and not flinch.

But give a blessing to one of these men.

The man runs for cover, cowering in the corner.

So many men are like that.

You may say, "We don't do that kind of thing in our family. Hugging and kissing is just not comfortable. I'm just not willing to do that. I just can't say it, and I can't touch them in love and tell them how I feel."

Then get ready to visit them in the state penitentiary.

Or maybe they'll just hate you.

Or maybe they'll become overachievers like Kirk Douglas, always trying to "prove" to the old man that they can do something worthwhile after all—but never really feeling quite "accepted" or "acceptable."

My old Browns coach, Blanton Collier, used to say, "Before you can improve, you must be willing to admit that you are wrong." He said that about a thousand times each season. He was also a great coach, the last one to lead the Browns to the

1964 NFL championship. Some people practice and practice and practice, but they practice their mistakes until they become bad habits. This happens in so many families.

We are afraid of the wrong things.

We are afraid to say the wrong things to our spouse and children, so we don't say anything at all.

We are afraid to appear weak, so we come on too strong, as in the strong, silent type. Who wants to live with the strong, silent type? You never know what they are thinking or feeling, and it puts everyone on edge.

We are afraid of something inside us; something a psychologist once called the bubble of emptiness. This grows in the heart and soul of every child who doesn't receive that well-done message, that feeling of being unconditionally loved, before the age of seven.

They need the blessing.

Some of us say, "I never got that, and I turned out OK."

Did you? Really? Be honest.

Do you have your own bubble of emptiness inside you? Have you been ignoring it? Have you tried to fill it with work? With sports? With stupid risk-taking? With sex? Drugs? Alcohol? Shopping? Eating? Could that be why so many of us have trouble making real friends, not just collecting acquaintances? Is that why there is a certain distance in our marriage, where the relationship is mostly a business deal?

Are we willing to subject our children to that same bubble of emptiness just because we are afraid to bless them? Because it may make us uncomfortable? Because we figure they can get along without it?

So many of us say we'll do anything for our kids to make their lives better.

Do we really mean that?

If so, then we have to bless them.

At this point, you should be saying, "If it's genuinely so pivotal . . . if it's the main cause of criminality . . . if it's the prime cause of insecurity, I can't afford to make such a major blunder. I must not allow my children to grow up twisted. They must not quiver inside, ravaged with insecurities. I would never forgive myself if I realized how crucial it is and then failed where my own kids needed me most! I want to bless my children."

I hope you're saying that.

But I fear some of you may say, "I don't feel like it."

There are a lot of things about being a parent, a spouse and a friend that we may not enjoy doing—but we do them because they are the right things to do. It starts with discipline and risking that uncomfortable feeling, but after a while, being a blesser blesses you back. Just stick with it. Parenting involves risks, but it's worth it. The alternative of creating, deep inner bubbles of emptiness is a downside risk you can't afford.

Some of us may need to take that approach. We need to realize faith is based on obedience, not feelings. In John 15:10, Jesus says if we love him, we'll obey his commandments. He didn't say,

"If you *feel* like it, obey my commandments."

When you step out in faith, when you obey God's Word and do what you *know* is right even when you don't *feel* like it, your feelings will follow. Real faith begins with obedience, not feelings. If we are doing the right thing, the feelings will follow. It may feel awkward or embarrassing now, but you'll reach a point where you won't just *know* you're doing the right thing, it will start to *feel* right. Feelings follow action. Don't delay. Don't think about it. Just start today and watch how God blesses you and your family.

PERSONAL APPLICATION AND PRAYER

✞ Most people aren't blessed! But everyone craves it.

✞ In the raging battles of life, don't miss the most important single point: Powerful, Positive Reinforcement.

✞ The bubble of emptiness must be broken through the "well done" message of love, value and belonging.

✞ "Suck it up" and ignore all the inner resistance to bless.

✞ Bless your loved ones even if you don't feel like it! Feelings follow obedience.

Prayer

*God, forgive me and all those who
influence me currently and have influenced
me in past generations when my world
seems to tilt away from blessing others.
God, help me just to "suck it up" and do it!
For Christ's sake, Amen.*

Chapter Four

WORDS DO MATTER

If you want to bless your children, you're going to discover two things:

It's easy.

It's hard.

It's easy because it can be done with a few words and a lot of love.

It's hard because some of us have never been blessed. Some of us not only struggle with words, but with love. We don't feel it. We don't know how to express it. We may even be afraid of it.

I'll start with the easy . . .

I have a little girl. Actually, she is not so little anymore, since she's grown and has her own children, but she's still my little girl. I did this when she was a child, and I do it today—I softly take her head in my hands, holding it behind her ears. My actions are slow, loving and gentle. As I look into her eyes, I say, "You're mine. You're a winner. I'm proud of you. I love you, and I think you're just right."

That's simple with my little girl. She's sweet, lovable, dainty, and I feel comfortable being tender. Yet some fathers have difficulty doing even that. Some fathers are afraid to touch and hug their older daughters. Some fathers don't realize how their girls—or their women—need that loving, protective touch. It should never be sexual or threatening in any way. I'm encouraging a father to tell his daughter that she will always be his *blessed daughter*, and nothing will ever change that.

I also have two boys. They weigh 280 and 290. They're both 6-foot-5, and they both played college football. One played pro ball. Though I played in the NFL, they're still bigger than me. I have to reach up to get to their ears. But I do it anyway, much the same way that I do with my daughter. I don't care if it looks stupid or feels strange. They need it. They want it. They may be adults, but they are still my sons.

I recently grabbed my eldest son and said, "You're mine and I'm glad. You're a winner and I'm proud of you. I love you, and I think you're terrific."

Tears welled up in his eyes and rolled down his checks. His shoulders began to shake.

He said, "I needed that, Dad."

They never get too old to need their parents' blessing: Grab them and hug them and kiss them.

In Genesis 27:26–27, Isaac said to his son Jacob, " 'Come here my son and kiss me' so he came near, and kissed him . . . and Isaac blessed his son."

Some may think Jacob was a little boy, but don't fall for it! He wasn't a little boy at all; he was an adult! Isaac was saying to a mature man, "Come close to me so that I might hug you and kiss you."

We never get too old to need our father and mother's affection. And you do it with a hug. It can't be done at a distance. When I bless my older son Billy, he's not some little boy. He's a man who played in the NFL, a father himself. He has kids of his own. He is a successful businessman in his middle forties. Yet he still needs his father's blessing.

In biblical times, the father's blessing was so critical, sons schemed to receive it. Genesis 27 tells the story of two boys, Esau and Jacob. Jacob was the younger. Esau, being the first son, should have received the birthright and the blessing. But Jacob was a con man. With his mother's help, he tricked Esau out of his birthright and his blessing. I can understand Esau being upset over losing the birthright (financial inheritance), but he was even more upset over losing the blessing. In Genesis 27:30–38, Esau weeps and pleads for the blessing. Four times in eight verses, Esau begs his father to bless him.

☦ Verse 34: ". . . he burst out with a loud and bitter cry and said to his father, 'Bless me—me too, my father!' "

✟ Verse 36: ". . . Haven't you reserved any blessing for me?"

✟ Verse 38a: " . . . 'Do you have only one blessing?'"

✟ Verse 38b: " 'Bless me too, my father!' Then Esau wept aloud."

Why is the blessing so important? Unless your father has blessed you, you don't feel like you're worth very much.

And every child needs it.

One of the biggest mistakes made by Isaac was to favor one child over the other. It's easy to do. Every child is different. Some are strong-willed; others want to please. Some are naturally happy; others are often depressed, seemingly for no reason. While we treat them all as individuals, we must bless them the same. If not, problems can be spread from one generation to the next. Consider what happened when Jacob became a father. He loved Joseph over all his other children. It was clear to everyone in the family that Joseph was indeed the favorite son. That led to Joseph's brothers resenting him and eventually selling him into slavery. He then landed in prison. The brothers told their father that Joseph had died. You can read about it starting in Genesis 37. Maybe that sounds like an extreme, but how many families put one sibling into a mental prison or treat someone in the family as if that person were dead? Sibling rivalry is dangerous and destructive, and parents can battle it by sincerely blessing each child, and doing it from the heart.

When I was in Florida years ago, I asked prison officials, "How many prisoners in Florida are Jewish?"

The answer was: thirteen.

Thirteen!

More than 60,000 inmates in prison in Florida at that time, and only thirteen were Jewish?

As of 2004, there were 585 Jewish inmates incarcerated in Florida. With a total prison population in Florida of 72,000, the Jewish inmates were still less than 1 percent, and Florida does have a significant Jewish population.

Why do so few Jews end up in jail? It's because many of the old Jewish fathers from the beginning of time followed the tradition of blessing their sons and daughters. Isaac wasn't the only one. It went down through the generations, and to this day, the Jewish father at the bar mitzvah blesses his son or daughter. That's why you don't see many Jews in prisons anywhere in the world. A lot of Gentiles, but few Jews. The old Jewish fathers know how to gather their sons and daughters close to them and hug them and kiss them and bless them! Many of us need to learn that practice. There are a lot of Baptists, Methodists, Pentecostals, Catholics and all denominations in prison—but very few Jews.

We were conducting a Weekend of Champions in Chicago at the Cook County Jail where 13,000 inmates are housed, and eighteen of them were still children, not yet teenagers. We asked those boys ages nine to twelve, "How many of you have carried a gun?"

All eighteen!

"How many of you have used drugs?"

All eighteen!

"How many of you are in a gang?"

All eighteen!

"How many of you have been sexually active?"

All eighteen!

"How many of you have a father that lives at home with you?"

Zero!

Do you wonder why they were in "lockup" for committing heinous crimes? It was because they had no father blessing them. In the last thirty-two years, I've been in more prisons than anyone who ever lived. I'm talking thousands of prisons, as we conducted our Weekend of Champions programs in around 400 prison units each year. I joke that I've been in prison so much since I retired from the NFL, I could rob a bank and wouldn't have to serve any time—I've already done it. My experience shows there is one thing that is so consistent that it has to be a major cause: When a man is a violent criminal, he usually had a weak, abusive or absentee father. The father cursed his own child to a life of crime.

In San Saba, Texas, at a prison for boys ranging from ten to fifteen years old, I asked the warden how many of these boys had a visit from their father in the last year.

You know what he told me?

One boy.

One boy got a fifteen-minute visit from his father. Only one boy out of 300 got a visit from his father. That's a tragedy. What happened to those other 299 fathers? I'll tell you what—they're a bunch of wimps! They're not fathers. They don't even deserve the title. They are just sperm donors. Real fathers don't desert their child just because he goes to prison. If your kid goes to prison, you visit him! God isn't done with that child yet, and neither are you. What is more important? That you have to deal with the embarrassment of a son or daughter in prison, or the support that son or daughter needs from you now more than ever? In fact, several studies have revealed that inmates who receive regular visits are less likely to return to prison than those who don't. The reason is obvious. They know they have a place to go and someone who still loves them.

Most major cities have runaway houses. When a kid runs away from home he or she can go to the runaway house, and they always try to talk the kid into calling home. Amazingly, the majority of the parents say, "We don't want them—you keep them."

When love is that temporary, no wonder they run away. In 68 percent of the cases, the parents don't want the kids back. No wonder they ran away in the first place!

The blessing has to be a way of life—consistently, no matter what! In the Wynne Unit in Huntsville, Texas, the inmates were used to enlarging the prisons in the 1950s. One man did a large part of the welding work as an inmate. He also was a father. The son of that welder/inmate was James Ryle, and he also was later incarcerated at that same Wynne Unit. James Ryle came to know the Lord in that prison. After his release, he attended seminary and later was pastor of the Vineyard Church in Longmont,

Colorado. He helped Bill McCartney found Promise Keepers.

James Ryle made an effort to find his father. When he did, they realized that his father was the welder who had built the prison cells where James had been incarcerated! A lot of fathers build cells for their sons by withholding the blessing. If it's not a physical prison cell, it can be bars around the hearts of our children. They can be held captive to insecurity. They can be trapped by a self-destructive drive to overachieve. They long to earn a blessing that can only be given.

Want to bless your children?

Then speak up!

It's essential to remember that a blessing must be said OUT LOUD. It's not just "understood." It must be spoken, not whispered. It must be sincere, not phony. It must be regular, not sporadic or done with a special agenda in mind.

This brings up one of my favorite stories. A guy was getting a divorce. During the divorce proceedings the judge asked, "How often do you tell your wife you love her?"

He said, "I told her the day I married her and that applies until I tell her differently." You wonder why he's getting a divorce?

I don't.

How could he be so irresponsible as to not say it out loud?

A bell isn't a bell until . . .

You ring it!

And a blessing isn't a blessing until . . . you say it!

"I know my daddy loved me—he just couldn't say it."

But if your daddy didn't say it, he really didn't bless you. By definition, a blessing has to be spoken.

It has to communicate three things:

✝ Love.

✝ Value.

✝ Belonging.

How do you start?

Very easy—you just say, "I love you."

You don't say, "I love you because . . ." Don't put any conditions on the love. If you tell your child that you love her because she's pretty or she's smart or she's a good athlete or actress, you are putting conditions on the love. You are loving the child for what she does, not who she is to you.

At the baptism of Jesus, God said, "This is my beloved Son in whom I am well pleased."

What a powerful, unmixed blessing.

You're not saying, "If you shape up and act right, then I'll love and bless you."

You're saying, "Even if you don't shape up and you don't act right, I'll still love you and bless you."

The blessing has absolutely nothing to do with your worthiness. It has everything to do with my unconditional love. Love that is conditional isn't love at all—it's a negotiation. Love has to be unconditional in order for it to be love.

In the story of the prodigal son in Luke 15, the son insulted his father, took his inheritance and went to a far country where he wasted the money on parties and women. He ended up in prison, a pigpen, and came to himself then he came home. When his father saw the boy coming from a great distance, he ran to meet him.

Did the father say, "I hope you've learned your lesson, boy!"

No, he gave him a robe and a ring and a hug and a kiss and an unconditional blessing. The Bible says that's what God is like. He loves us unconditionally, having nothing to do with our worthiness. That's what every human father and mother should be like. When the child moves toward repentance, the real father runs to meet him. In Luke 15:22, the father restores the son to his original place in the family: "Bring out the best robe and put it on him. Put a ring on his finger and sandals on his feet." The father ordered a feast and celebration to begin. He celebrated "my son who was lost is now found." His jealous older brother wanted to talk about how the lost son wasted money on whores and drunken binges, along with his brother's other sins. The father focused on love and forgiveness and the blessing.

So a parent must say, "I love you. You're terrific."

That's unconditional love and value.

Then you say, "You're mine!"

That's belonging.

You may even want to add, "And I will always love you and you will always be mine, no matter what!"

Don't we all long to hear that kind of message from someone close to us? If we don't get it at home, we'll look for it somewhere else. That's why some people bury themselves in work. They do well on the job and receive a blessing in the form of promotions, raises and praise from their bosses. It's not the right blessing because it's based on performance, but it's better than nothing. At least the gang at the office appreciates you, right?

We all want someone to love and value us.

Why do kids join street gangs? Because they didn't belong to that most important gang of all—"the family." Often you'll see teardrops tattooed on the face of a gang member. Those drops indicate the entry fee to the gang. Perhaps they murdered someone or committed another heinous initiation ritual that had to be performed to become a full-fledged "gangbanger."

Some people are so desperate for a blessing, they will kill for it!

Whose job is it to make the child feel that he belongs to the family?

It's the father's job.

No mother can do this alone. Inmates on death row invariably love their mamas. It's the dads they have the problem with—it's the dads they hate! Ideally, it takes both parents to make children feel that they belong. Dad, you must make the children feel that you're proud of them, that they are yours. Mom needs help in making the child feel that sense of belonging. The poor single mother is fighting a major battle in rearing children with no father in the home.

There also needs to be a touch. A hug. A physical connection that expresses protection and belonging.

Some people say, "We just don't hug in our family."

Fine, get ready to visit your child in jail, where you won't have to worry about hugging. You'll talk on a telephone with a piece of glass between you. I've seen parents touch the glass with their hands, their children touching the other side of the glass—one hand trying to reach another, but the jail glass keeping them apart. I bet they wished they had hugged their children more when they could, when they were young. Or get ready to have an adult child who doesn't hug you when you need it. Or a son or daughter who is never quite sure how they feel about you— because you never made it clear how much you loved them. People can be living in the free world, but still wandering around in their own mental and spiritual prisons.

I'm not suggesting there is ever an excuse for turning the blessing into a form of sexual abuse. Everyone knows the difference between the healthy hug and the unhealthy type. It must be done carefully. The real man and the real woman will look directly into their eyes (unblinking) while touching them in a warm manner. A touch to the face is a great deal more intimate than a touch on the shoulder. I have some rules for blessing in order to keep my loved ones from feeling uncomfortable. With my daughters-in-law, I only kiss their foreheads. I hug them with an A-frame hug and kiss them on the forehead or on the hand while verbally speaking a blessing to them. I don't want it to seem sexual in any way, but warm and close without invading their space.

For my daughter, I kiss her lightly on the lips and hug her as well. I'm afraid to kiss my daughters-in-law on the mouth because it could make them uncomfortable. I think the blessing should never make the person being blessed uncomfortable. You have to earn your right to bless. If you've been grouchy and controlling or unloving and then you try to cover it by a meaningless blessing, it has little impact. What you say and do all the time is most important. Then the blessing becomes the extension of the pattern of your lifetime.

Parents must earn the right by being open, close, affirming and never delivering the put-down. Abusive discipline— "I'm determined to teach that boy something"—no matter how well meaning doesn't fly.

In *Chicken Soup for the Father's Soul,* John Trent wrote about a father who decided he was going to take his daughters on a "date with Dad" every week. He had a ten-year-old, a nine-year-old and a two-year-old. He'd take the nine- and ten-year-old every week. They would come home after their "date with Dad" and brag about it.

The two-year-old said, "Why can't I go?"

He explained, "Darling, you're only two and you need to be three before you can go."

She demanded, "I'm two-and-a-half and I want to go right now!"

He said, "Okay."

He took her down to the local McDonalds, bought Egg McMuffins and put them on the table between them. Then he grabbed her by her pudgy little hands, pulled her across the table closer to him and said, "You're mine and I'm glad. You're a winner and I'm proud of you. I love you and I think you're terrific."

When he tried to pull his hands away to eat his breakfast, she said, "More, Daddy, more!"

So he said, "You get along so well with your friends, you obey your mother so well, and you play so well with your sisters."

Then he tried to pull his hands away again and she said, "Longer, Daddy, longer!"

Aren't we all like that?

Don't we all want a blessing? More words from those who love us?

As parents, we need to bless children, not curse them. They long for more love, more affirmation—more and longer and longer periods of encouragement and less of instruction.

So what's the well done message?

"You're mine, I love you, you're terrific and you're just what I want you to be."

You've got to say it out loud. You have to mean it. You have to realize it's not a formula that when repeated works some magic; it's how God expects fathers to relate to their children.

As Paul wrote in Philippians 4:8: "Whatever is right, whatever is noble, whatever is pure, whatever is lovely, whatever is admirable—if anything is excellent or praiseworthy—think about such things."

Let's take this another step: We should not just think the words in this positive way, but say them out loud. Remember to say them to our children. Words are never empty when they reveal our true attitudes and actions.

PERSONAL APPLICATION AND PRAYER

☦ Adult children continue to need blessing.

☦ Start blessing in the fetal stage.

☦ A date with Dad is great for kids!

☦ Even Bible characters (Esau and Jacob and Joseph and his brothers) battled for blessing. It continues to this day.

☦ The search for belonging is why kids join gangs.

☦ The verbal blessing must include love, value and belonging!

☦ Be certain that the blessing is equal, even with in-laws.

☦ Earn the right to bless.

☦ Blessing is simply an extension of the habit pattern of a lifetime. Don't try to cover up weak parenting by superficial hugs and kisses.

☦ Don't make the one you are blessing uncomfortable. Move slowly and naturally toward a more natural hug and kiss. With my daughter, it's gently on the lips. With my daughters-in-law, it's a kiss on the forehead. It's a hug and a pat on the back with my son-in-law.

PRAYER

Oh God, help me to be skillful in blessing—
doing it unapologetically, but not making them feel
uncomfortable; always sincerely, but never
to make up for foolish mistakes.
For Christ's sake, Amen.

Chapter Five

EVERY CHILD
DESERVES A BLESSING

When my first grandson was born, I had dreams.

Dreams that he could become president.

Dreams that he could play pro football like his father and grandfather.

Dreams that he'd be smart and used mightily by God, that he would make his mark.

I had so many dreams for Billy Ray Glass.

I even had dreams that I'd be a better grandfather to Billy Ray than I was a father to my own children. I had figured some things out. I had grown and matured. I had made some mistakes with my own children, but I wouldn't do the same with Billy Ray. I knew my grandson would have so much going for him. His father and mother were terrific people. My wife, Mavis, and I couldn't wait to be grandparents. He'd be the perfect boy born into the perfect family. God was blessing us, I just knew it. But like so much in life, I didn't know a thing. On the second day of his life, we discovered he had Down's syndrome. That meant he could never be president. He'd never play in the NFL or even on his high school team. He'd never be a great writer or speaker or pastor or anything else we may have dared to dream.

Now he'd be considered a "special needs" child. We were crushed.

Mavis kept a journal and wrote, "When the doctors told us, I couldn't do anything but stare. This couldn't be happening. Laura (my daughter in-law) hadn't even taken an aspirin during her pregnancy. Later, doctors would tell us that it wasn't anything that anyone did, it was simply 'a genetic accident.' I was devastated. I couldn't think. My joy disintegrated into deep sorrow. Doctors told us that some parents choose not to see their babies, but just 'put them away' in an institution . . . my mind was reeling. Why? What did I do wrong? Maybe I didn't pray enough. Maybe I was being punished for something. And Billy and Laura, how could they take this?"

I felt the same as Mavis: cheated and angry.

As Mavis later wrote, "It's God's fault. I prayed every day for Laura to have an easy birth and a perfect baby. I got a NO and NO in answer to both of those prayers. I had never gotten such distinct NO answers to prayer about something so important."

Haven't we all felt like that at some point? Like our prayers bounced off the ceiling and came back to us marked "Return to Sender?" Every child is supposed to be a blessing. Right?

The amazing thing was the reaction of Laura and Billy, the parents.

Ten minutes after hearing what was wrong with Billy Ray, Laura said, "Bring me my baby!" She held that child like a loving mother would any child. Billy was strong. He kept saying, "This is *exactly* the child God wants us to have. He is *perfect.*"

My son did cry during those first few nights, but he blessed that child every day.

We also began to realize how God had blessed us, how our children had all been big, healthy, strong, smart and perfect, at least in our eyes.

But God was about to do something else with Billy Ray. As he began to grow, I noticed something wonderful about him. He had an unusual amount of love. Every time he'd come over to the house, he'd get on my lap and hug me and kiss me and talk to me, and sometimes he'd sit in my lap for ten or fifteen minutes. If I got ten to fifteen seconds of his "normal" little brother's time, I was lucky. But Billy Ray had all the time in the world for "Gams-Gams."

That's me: "Gams-Gams."

The moment I entered the house, he'd start yelling, "Gams-Gams." When he was young, I went to his house. He was on the floor, playing with his toy cars going, "Udden-udden, udden-udden."

I smiled.

He went, "Udden-udden."

I smiled again.

So, real loud, he screamed, "Udden-udden!"

Finally, I got the picture. He wanted me to play, "Udden-udden."

So I got down on one knee and I took another toy car.

I said, "Udden-udden."

He liked that pretty well, but I was just down on one knee. He was on his belly. He wanted me down on my belly? I wasn't sure. I was in a full dress suit and I didn't really want to get on my belly.

But Billy Ray wanted Gams-Gams on his belly to play udden-udden.

So I went spread-eagle on the floor, yelling, "Udden-udden."

He was yelling, "Udden-udden."

And we were having a wonderful time playing udden-udden.

Some friends of my son came in. They had to step over me to get into the room and they said, "Oh, Mr. Glass, we've always wanted to meet you."

They put their hands out to shake hands with me, but I was yelling, "Udden-udden."

I didn't even stop to shake hands with them. If they didn't like it, you know how much I cared? Zero! No man stands quite as tall as when he gets on his knees—or even on his belly—with his little son or grandson or little daughter or granddaughter.

I was more concerned about blessing my grandson with my time by playing his game than by impressing strangers. Billy Ray has taught me that no man or woman is ever so much the fool as when they think they're too tough and too big and too macho to do it. The reason I tell the udden-udden story is there are times to bless those we love when it's not convenient, when we may even look stupid. But who are we really trying to impress? The people closest to us, or those whom we just met? Too often, we are more concerned with blessing strangers and business associates with our time and words than those in our own family.

We've all been guilty of that. We all need an udden-udden attitude, an attitude of humility. Sometimes that starts with our kids. We may look back at how we raised our children and realize that in some areas, we blew it. Maybe they seemed hard to bless. Maybe they weren't what we dreamed. Maybe they even let us down. Maybe we think God didn't hold up his end of the bargain because of how our children turned out.

Some people may see Billy Ray that way.

That's because they don't know Billy Ray.

Is Billy Ray hard to bless?

Here's what his father wrote to me:

"Dad, I believe they are easier to bless. What I really secretly believe is that they don't need my blessing at all. They are in contact with the Savior. It is Billy Ray's love that I seek, which means that I only have to be in his presence! That's all that is required! He is my guide, my teacher, the one who recharges my love battery, enabling me to love others. Don't miss this, Dad! This is what God has done!

People like Billy Ray are put among us to show us how to love."

When we fail—and we all do—we need to start fresh. Get an udden-udden attitude. Tell that person that we know we have hurt him/her by holding back the blessing. We need to say, "I messed up. Will you forgive me? Will you give me a second chance? Will you give me the chance to be the good daddy, mommy or grandparent that you need? It's not easy to admit failure to those closest to us. I want to bless you and do it biblically. I want to do it with a hug, and I want to say it out loud. I want you to know that I love you unconditionally. I want to make you feel like you're mine and I really do love you and you are terrific!"

Billy Ray is now twenty-two years old and very much a mature, young man. In spite of his Down's syndrome, he functions very well. During his high school years, he was so involved with the entire student body, his brothers insisted he was one of the most popular kids in school. It's because he loved everyone, hugged them and was very positive with them. Often, children with Down's syndrome are very loving regardless of their environment. Laura says it's because they are angels, and I think she is right.

He loves football, and he was a part of the team. I'd ask him what he did with the team and he'd say proudly, "I'm the water boy."

He served as water boy for his 5A team all the way to the state championship. He proudly wears a state championship ring. He took his job very seriously. In my opinion, he was the best water boy in the history of Carroll High School.

During basketball season, Billy Ray would run out to mid-court with a bag of basketballs and heave them with all his might at the rim. Once he sank three out of four from midcourt. The crowd went wild. He turned in a circle with his hands raised high in the air like a champion wrestler. But there have been times when he presented some unique challenges. His mother recently told me with tears in her eyes, "The blessings so far outweigh the problems that it isn't even comparable!"

Everybody in the family knew she was right.

Billy Ray arranged for me to speak at his school. He went to the coaches and told them of my NFL days. He introduced me in front of the huge pep rally crowd in the school gym. He seemed totally relaxed and made himself understood. I was so proud to see him speak so well in public because several surveys have revealed public speaking is one of the greatest fears for most people. Billy Ray didn't seem to care, he was just his loving, giving self.

Here's how his father sees Billy Ray:

> *"He takes everything I say to him literally. If I said, 'Don't go into that dark room because, Billy, if you do, the boogeyman will jump out from under the bed and eat you,' Billy Ray believes me. Of course, I wouldn't say that to him because I wouldn't want to frighten him, but you have to understand he believes everything that I tell him, both good and bad. So if I tell him I am proud of*

him and love him very much, he also totally believes that I love him! Which I do! As our intellect grows, our ability to trust diminishes. My blessing strategy with Billy is really quite easy compared to our other sons Matthew (20) and Joshua (17).

"Billy Ray being our firstborn was really great for my spiritual and mental growth as a father. I laugh as I write these words. When he was born, I would have thought I would never be able to say such a thing. The initial pain that Laura and I felt when our physician told us that our son had Down's syndrome was unbearable. I understate the pain and emotional complexity of that situation. Jesus makes all things possible, doesn't he? Easy to say, twenty-two years later. Matthew and Joshua were born after Billy Ray. Matthew is our second son and Joshua is our third son. Matthew, of course, means 'Gift of God,' and Joshua was sent by Moses to investigate the Promised Land while the children of Israel wandered in the desert for forty years. The boys know that their names are blessings because they themselves were named after those great men in scripture. They know that their father named them. I used their names to reinforce their blessing!

"From the time the boys were old enough to listen to Bible stories, I would read so they'd know they are blessed. I would hold them and say to them, 'And do you know who else is called Joshua?' My Joshua would look up at me and say with a huge smile, 'ME.' 'That's right,' I agreed! 'Joshua,' I would say, 'you are very special to me! I thought for a long time while your mother was pregnant about what to name you. I decided to name you

Joshua, and do you know why? Joshua would remember the deeds of the biblical character and tell how he thought his own character traits were like those of Moses' right-hand man.'"

While I learned a lot about blessing from my father, having Billy Ray took it to another level. We realize how he blesses us back. Billy Ray is generous. He loans money to his brothers because they usually don't have any, and he has a big bank account from all of his jobs. However, they went too far and started to take advantage of his generosity. When he realized what was happening, he cut them off and now refuses to loan them any money. He doesn't appear to have any big hang-ups with the fact that he's Down's. He loves to participate in the Special Olympics and displays his medals and trophies proudly in his room. He lives at home with his parents, but dreams of someday getting married. He is very interested in girls and has a girlfriend. Recently, he took his girlfriend on a date. His parents accompanied them! They ordered spaghetti. They met at special education class, and they were having the time of their lives eating spaghetti—simply giggling and having fun. After dinner, their parents dropped them off at a movie and picked them up later. At the end of the evening, Billy Ray escorted his date to the door, told her how much he enjoyed it, how much fun they'd had and kissed her good night. He returned to the car and sat smiling next to his dad in the front seat while his mother sat in the back.

His father asked Billy, "What are you thinking about?"

Billy Ray said, "I was thinking I have a wonderful life!"

He does in fact have a wonderful life. He works at what he considers to be three important jobs. He's a busboy at CiCi's Pizza. He is a volunteer at the police station where he mostly hangs around with the officers whom he really loves. He also works another job as a busboy at a big restaurant.

I recently asked him, "Billy Ray, what do you do?"

He said, "I'm a busboy!"

He said it like he was coach of the Dallas Cowboys. He was very proud of himself.

Some people may have considered him a "genetic accident."

We know better.

It wasn't that our family chose to bless Billy Ray—it was really that we were blessed by God who gave us this angel-like person. The truth is we did nothing but receive the gift of Billy Ray. He stayed in high school until he was twenty-one, as the law allows for special needs students. That was good because there have been so many teachers who have worked so hard to help Billy Ray learn and grow. Now he is twenty-two and still living with his parents.

"We know he will never live on his own," said his father. "He can't. But that's OK because I just don't want him to ever leave me. We know he'll never be like a lot of other men his age. He's actually better. He understands more than I do. Maybe his IQ's low but he understands all of the things that count, and those things are his complete focus."

Here's what I say when I bless him, "Billy Ray, you are mine and you are special and you are terrific and I love you and I'll always love you."

No one loves us back better or stronger than Billy Ray.

And he blesses us back in ways we've never imagined, ways that his brother and most other children will never be able to do. Like his dad says, "Just being in his presence is a blessing."

PERSONAL APPLICATION AND PRAYER

✝ Dealing with a Down's syndrome grandson was my challenge. What's your personal challenge?

✝ What happens when God answers "No!" to two prayers in a row? You trust in God and wait for the message that will change your life.

✝ What is your unexpected blessing? Mine was Billy Ray!

✝ The great value of an udden-udden attitude—humility—gets you right with God and man.

✝ Naming children helps to shape their lives.

✝ Learn from those who can teach you. I learned from Billy Ray, who isn't like other men his age. He focuses on what really counts!

PRAYER

God, thank you for an angel sent from heaven
to help us focus on what really counts!
For Christ's sake, Amen!

Chapter Six

THE SECRET
TO THE BLESSING

Some people have told me, "I've never been blessed, so how am I supposed to bless anyone else?"

It's a legitimate question, but it's not an excuse. Suppose you are a doctor, a lawyer, a dentist, an accountant, a teacher or a salesman. And suppose you are the first in your family to have that kind of job. Did you say, "How can I be a doctor when I never had a doctor for a mother or father?"

No, you learned how to be a doctor. You studied. You made friends and gained role models in the medical field. You weren't about to let your less-than-ideal experience in the medical field stop you from reaching your dream.

So how do you learn to bless your children?

You start by setting your mind to do it, by deciding this is important, that it means as much to you as your career.

That is more than enough motivation to take some difficult, but necessary steps.

But then realize something else—this is a spiritual matter. The God who created the universe, the God who sent his son to die for your sins, the God who has heaven waiting for anyone who is willing to come to him with an open heart and the desire to confess sins and be healed, will do more than help you bless your children.

God wants to bless you!

That may be harder for some of you to believe than the concept of you extending that blessing to your children.

God wants to bless you!

Think about that.

Your father may not have blessed you. Your mother may not have blessed you. Your family may have done nothing but curse you.

God wants to bless you!

Are you willing to receive it? Are you willing to take it on faith that God is ready to bless you? And can you extend that blessing to others?

I hate it when I hear, "You can't teach an old dog new tricks."

Since when are any of us old dogs? Besides, if you've ever had dogs, you know they can always keep learning.

Just like we can.

There are times when we just have to change, when God brings things into our lives that force us to change. I broke into the NFL with the Detroit Lions and had established myself as a pretty good defensive end. I had no interest in being traded, didn't think I deserved to be traded and certainly was shocked when I heard I was traded to Cleveland along with Jim Ninowski and Hopalong Cassidy for Milt Plum, Tommy Watkins and Dave Lloyd. Even worse, I heard about the trade first from Detroit sportswriter and good friend, Watson Spoelstra. An hour after he gave me the news, Detroit head coach George Wilson informed me of the deal. I could have been insulted because a sportswriter told me first; the team should have had the decency to immediately inform me of something so critical to my future and my family. I could have said, "I don't want to go to Cleveland." Of course, I knew the answer to that. If I didn't want to play for Cleveland, then I wasn't going to play anywhere.

When I talked to Cleveland coach Paul Brown, I couldn't say, "Coach, the Detroit Lions wear beautiful blue uniforms. The Cleveland Browns wear drab brown jerseys. I'll play for your team, but I want to keep wearing those blue Detroit uniforms. I'm more comfortable in that color."

None of us would dare say anything like that, at least not if we expected to keep our jobs. We do what the bosses tell us to do, wear what they say to wear and act as they tell us to act. That's part of what it means to work. It's called adjusting. It's the same thing in the Christian life.

You can tell me, "I don't feel comfortable blessing my children."
I say, "Do it anyway."

More importantly, the Bible says it. Ephesians 6:4 commands us: "Fathers, do not exasperate your children."

In the book of Philippians, Paul writes that we should encourage each other, which is another way of saying we should bless other people. When I sign my name or give autographs to fans, next to my signature I add this verse, Philippians 1:3, which reads, "I thank God every time I remember you."

I want people to look up that verse and feel blessed. As Paul writes in Philippians 2:14: "Do everything without complaining or arguing." I suggest everyone read the entire book of Philippians and remember that Paul wrote it from prison. Throughout its four short chapters, he is calling us to do something that won't come easy, something that we all must do: bless those we love and those who are important to us—just as God blesses us.

If your boss insisted on a positive attitude and your job depended on taking that approach, most of us would work very hard to do it.

In fact, it is amazing what we can do when we see no other choice.

I played football for twenty-two seasons, ten as an amateur, twelve as a pro. That's twenty-two training camps. No player likes training camp. It's nothing but practice, drills, sprints, sweat, sprains, aches and exhaustion. I've grown sore, been knocked unconscious, strained ligaments, sprained ankles and had severe cuts. I bled a few times each week. But I knew that it was the only way to get in shape, and to play in the regular season, I needed to spend six weeks in that training camp doing things I didn't want to do. After winning a championship or having a good season, the joy that comes erases any pain from training camp. If I didn't suffer, then I would not have grown as a player. I also brainwashed myself. I kept focusing on the positive when it came to training camp, how it was making me a better player, a stronger person, and bringing me closer to my teammates. People are amazed when I tell them that I never missed a practice in twenty-two years. I'd tell myself that I don't get sore like the other guys, that I was gaining momentum which would lead to a great season and give me a tremendous advantage over the other players in the NFL.

After a while, I really did believe it.

It also was true. You do play how you practice, so I made sure to practice well—and enjoy it as much as possible.

It's the same with the blessing.

A lot of fathers need to go to their first spiritual training camp. Some need to learn new techniques. I spent the first few months of my rookie pro career as a left defensive end. It was my comfort zone. When I lined up, my left hand was on the ground, my left foot was back. To me, that stance was automatic. I did it like I brushed my teeth, the same way, same technique, every day. But I was soon moved to right defensive end. That may not sound like a big deal to most people, but instead of my left hand on the ground, it was my right. Instead of my left foot back, it was my right.

In the beginning, everything felt awkward. For some of us, the blessing will be like that. We didn't get it from anyone else, we're not used to doing it and we wonder if anything good will come from it. Some of us will say, "OK, I switched from my blue uniform to the brown uniform, isn't that enough?"

That's like saying, "OK, I came to Christ. I believe he died for my sins and rose from the dead. I accept him as my Lord and Savior. I am doing a much better job in how I deal with my family and live my life, isn't that enough?"

Not if you want your children to receive God's full blessing on their lives. It's up to you to deliver it, and if that means changing hands and spiritually standing a new way, then do it! If your boss told you to do something or lose your job, wouldn't you give it a sincere effort? Aren't your children worth more than your job? If not, then you need to examine that part of your life. Everyone can learn new things—whether it's a different stance at defensive end or another approach to our children. If I wanted to keep playing for the Cleveland Browns, then I needed to adapt to that new position and work extra hard to feel natural there. I did it. You can do it with your family.

Hall of Fame coach Vince Lombardi used to say, "Potential means you ain't done nothing yet."

All of us have potential. God's not done with any of us yet.

Ex-con, ex-NFL player, doctor, accountant, teacher, lawyer, millionaire or a hardworking blue-collar guy—it doesn't matter who you are today or who you were in the past. The real question is what kind of father will you become?

And that starts with this question: What have you done about Jesus? It's not what church you attended as a child or what church your mother happens to be a member of or how your grandfather was a preacher.

Nor does it have anything to do with the fact that the only church some families attend on Sundays is the high church of the National Football League, where they arrive at the stadium parking lot at the crack of dawn, then break open the beer and throw the burgers on the grill.

It's not about what your family did with church.

It's not about how you were (or weren't) introduced to God as a child.

It's not about how the blessing was handled in your family.

It's about you and God.

How each of us deals with God often determines how we bless our children.

For those of us who are Christians, the Bible tells us in 2 Corinthians 5:17, "If anyone is in Christ, he is a new creation. The old is gone, the new has come."

That's why you can bless your children, even if you've never felt the blessing of your earthly father. It starts with a relationship between God and each of us.

You don't *feel* like blessing your children?

Feelings can be tricky. How many of us feel like going to work, paying taxes, going to the doctor or even changing our infant's diapers? But we do it because it's the right thing to do. Faith is based first on obedience, not feelings. What happens is, as we walk in faith and trust and obey as the old hymn commands, our feelings catch up. What was strange begins to feel natural and right.

According to Ezekiel 36:26, God says, "A new heart I will give you, and a new spirit I'll put within you."

I overheard two men talking about a celebrity who was involved in a scandal. One of them said, "That guy, he's going to stand before God one day, and he's going to give an account!"

They were angry.

I said, "You're right, he will. But so will you! And so will I! Forget that guy. You don't have to answer for him. You have to answer for you!"

The reason people want to talk about someone whom they consider a worse sinner is because they don't want to think about themselves. My attitude is that I don't have to answer for you. I do have to answer for me.

When we die, God will ask each of us: "What did you do with my son, Jesus?"

That's the pertinent question. When you answer that one properly, the others fall in line. God's not going to ask you on Judgment Day, "Did you do this or that, which was wrong?"

The only unforgivable sin is the sin of disbelief, to refuse to believe and follow Christ.

Want to know why some of us can't bless our children? It's because we can't believe God will bless us. This often happens when we can't forgive ourselves for something that we did or forgive someone else for something they did to us. Sometimes we end up thinking God is mad at us or we are angry at God. There are times when some of us feel all these things at once!

We can't forgive ourselves, and we can't forgive someone else.

We think God is mad at us, and we have some issues with God.

We are hurt, angry, confused.

No wonder some of us are intimidated by the idea of the blessing. It's why some of us need to straighten out our relationship with God before we do anything else.

Remember, it's not about our own fathers, who didn't bless us, or anyone else. It's about each of us and God. It's admitting we are sinners, that we need a Savior. It's believing Jesus died for our sins. It's a free ticket to heaven! But it's more. It's the key to getting past that roadblock of blessing our children. It's how we learn and accept forgiveness for our own sins, which helps us forgive others. It's how we may be able to forgive our own earthly fathers for not blessing us and forgive ourselves if we didn't bless some of our children. It's coming to a critical realization that our earthly father is not our Heavenly Father.

An inmate recently told me, "My old man's been dead for twenty years. I hate him so badly that in my imagination I dig him up from the dead every morning and beat him to death again!"

I said, "Why don't you go to his grave in your imagination and forgive him and get on with your life? Put it behind you. If you continue to hate him, he'll continue to ruin your life even though he's dead. I repeat, go to his grave in your imagination and forgive him and put it behind you and go on with your life!"

Then he needs to find someone to bless him. I tell people, "If your father is alive, ask for his blessing. If he refuses, go and find someone who will. If he's dead, forgive him and put it behind you and go on. Put it behind you once and for all and find someone who will bless you."

A lot of us need to forgive a parent before we can come into the true blessing God has for us. I recently talked to an inmate who was twenty-seven. He said he first met me when he was fourteen. He was in a men's prison, despite being a juvenile. I talked to him while he was in solitary confinement. At first, I didn't remember him. I meet so many young men each year. But as he told me about his case, his situation came back to me. When he was fourteen, he was part of a robbery that went bad. I don't recall all the details, but he shot three people and two of them died. He said he came to Christ when I talked to him in that cell when he was fourteen. That made me feel great to know I was a small, good part of his tortured past.

Then he said, "I've heard you speak nine times on the Weekend of Champions. Each time, it was about the blessing."

I believed that, because I usually talk about the blessing to inmates. I give the message hundreds of times each year.

"But I needed to hear it nine times to finally understand it," he said. "Only now am I starting to get it. My father committed suicide. Then I got into a gang. In less than a year, my life fell apart and I was in prison."

He was searching for his father's blessing from that gang, he just didn't know it. I've met a lot of inmates whose fathers committed suicide. They feel rejected, abandoned and worthless. Their father didn't even think enough of them to stay alive and watch them grow up. At least that's how they see it. That made sense to me. Research tells us that suicide is one of the worst curses a parent can inflict on a family. It's very common for a suicide to appear in several different generations. It was true in the family of Ernest Hemingway. The father of the great writer killed himself. So did Hemingway. So did one of Hemingway's children.

If only Hemingway could have understood the impact of Psalm 147:3: "[God] heals the brokenhearted and binds up their wounds."

It doesn't say we will never be hurt again. It says our hearts can be healed, our physical wounds bandaged up. I compare it to surgery. Most of the time, there is a scar that lasts a lifetime after any significant operation. But the pain is nothing like it was before the surgery. As the years pass, the scars grow smaller and smaller—unless we keep picking at them. Then they could get infected, and the pain is worse than ever.

Here's the point: Sometimes we have to do some surgery in our own families. We have to cut out a person who continually abuses us, a person who has no sense of repentance or any desire to change. Forgiving that person means turning them over to

God and releasing ourselves from the power they once held over us. Forgiving means no longer thinking about them, replaying past events or old conversations. It's allowing God to deal with them in his own way and his own time. It's surrendering our own natural desire to get even and remembering that the Bible tells us in Romans 12:19: "Do not take revenge, my friends, but leave room for God's wrath. For it is written, 'It is mine to avenge, I will repay,' says the Lord."

We can forgive an abusive person, trusting God to handle the battle for us. But we do not have to bring a dangerous person back into our lives. We move on to see what God has planned for us. Once that happens, once we separate the earthly father who abandoned or hurt us, we move to a Heavenly Father who wants to forgive us and bring us into a close relationship with him.

We begin to say, "I may never get the blessing of my earthly father, but I can always get the blessing of my Heavenly Father."

But the truth is, I need both.

So how does that happen when your earthly father can't or won't bless you?

God has an answer for that.

PERSONAL APPLICATION AND PRAYER

✝ Not being blessed by your parents doesn't negate your responsibility of blessing your loved ones.

✝ Blessing your children isn't optional! It is the command of scripture. Those who are blessed thrive, and those who aren't suffer.

✝ Change is never easy, whether it is something so small as moving from left to right defensive end or so pivotal as blessing your loved ones. It is still difficult. Nevertheless, it is infinitely important!

✝ In that great Judgment Day you are accountable before God for yourself. Get right with God first and then with all your loved ones.

✝ Your Heavenly Father and your earthly father aren't the same. Stop confusing the two.

✝ Go to your father and ask for his blessing. If he's dead, go to his grave in your imagination and forgive him and put it behind you and go on with your life. Maybe your father ruined your life while he was alive, but don't allow him to continue to ruin your life even after he is dead. Again, forgive him. Put it behind you and go on with your life!

PRAYER

*Oh God, help me to forgive those
who have hurt me. I confess where I have
been wrong and claim I John 1:9,
"If we confess our sins, He is faithful and
just and will forgive us our sins and purify
us from all unrighteousness."
For Christ's sake, Amen.*

Chapter Seven

BATTLING REJECTION
WITH A BLESSING

So many of us miss our fathers.

Sometimes, they've passed away. Other times, they're still alive but in our minds, they are gone. My own father has been dead for fifty years. He's buried at Seaside Cemetery in Corpus Christi, Texas.

I still miss him and I'm not ashamed to say it.

Telling me that I was loved no matter what was a part of his daily routine, only he made me feel special every time he did it. Hugging and kissing me came natural to him. Blessing has always been easy for me because it was for him. He would rub my back or head and pray with me. I never remember a negative word from him.

He died when I was fourteen.

In high school, I missed him the most after football games. Our team bus would arrive back at the field house either wild with joy after a victory or sad with defeat. It seemed every other player had a dad waiting to pick him up after the game. The dads would be lining both sides of the field house driveway beside our dressing room. My sweet mother and younger sister were always there.

But I still I missed my dad.

If only he'd seen me play for the Cleveland Browns in the 1964 NFL Championship game when we upset Baltimore, 27–0. Or if he had seen me in one of the four Pro Bowls. Or when I played at Baylor. Or when I grew into a good player during my senior year in high school. Or when my ministry took off with the Weekend of Champions in various prisons or during some of our citywide crusades. Or to meet my wife, my children, my grandchildren.

My father never demanded that I perform for him; he wisely blessed me simply because I was his son. He understood the heart of the blessing. But I wanted him to see the kind of man that I'd become, that I turned out okay because he had blessed me when there was nothing much to bless. He blessed me for only one reason—I was his son! I wish I had gotten one of his big hugs after a game. I'm sure he had a better view from heaven's grandstand, but I needed someone with skin on to be my father.

The most horrible time of my young life was watching his strong body shrink.

Some of you may have seen that happen to someone you love—they get physically smaller in front of your eyes. It usually happens when they grow older. But my father was forty-three years old, a former minor-league pitcher who carried 205 pounds on his six-foot frame. He was the essence of strength and health to me.

Then came Hodgkin's disease.

He shriveled from that muscular 205 to a 140-pound skeleton, and I watched it happen over the last two years of his life. When my dad was told he had Hodgkin's disease, he never believed he would die like he did. He prayed for the Lord's healing. After his death, I read through his well-worn Bible and found every passage about healing underlined. I heard him say to my weeping mother, "My doctor tells me if I can just hang on for a few years, they'll find a cure."

They did—about twenty years after his death. Now Hodgkin's patients live a near normal life span. But what my father endured was so agonizing, so destructive, so physically debilitating, it has haunted my memory for fifty years. His joints lost their lubricants, meaning every move brought unbearable pain. Heat helped a little. He asked me to get him hot towels. For hours, I'd run back and forth between the bathtub filled with hot water and soaking towels. I'd wring them out and dash at top speed to his reclining chair in the living room. I vividly remember burning my hands as I'd wring out those towels and then running as fast as I could so I could hand them to him before they cooled off.

It was all I could do for him, and I knew it wasn't much.

But my father considered it a blessing, and he blessed me for it. He'd repeat to my mother or anyone else who might be in the room, "William always gets the towels hotter than anyone."

It felt so good to think I was helping him. Fifty years have come and gone, but I still feel the satisfaction of my deep need for blessing being fulfilled in such a unique way. This blessing was my only blessing in the last two years of his life. He was too sick to come to my room for his blessing ritual. I missed his nightly visits to my bedside to talk and pray with me. I missed his constant blessings. It began to dawn on me even in my teens that a father's blessing has an almost mystical power. When he was there, "all was right with the world." I needed my dad to help establish my identity. For years, I floated, not knowing who or what I was—my dad was not there to tell me. I couldn't figure it out. I was in a haze.

This is a common problem.

Consider that Jesus did little of importance until his blessing at his baptism. He was tempted just as we are tempted (Heb. 4:15). He certainly must have been tempted at the crucial point of identity. Since he had no earthly father, he could have had no Bar Mitzvah. Joseph would not have the right to give Jesus a bar mitzvah because only the father can give bar mitzvah. Jesus knew God was his father. But he was also human, and he must have asked, "Am I God or man?" Throughout his life, Christ was attacked by Satan at this point of identity. "If you are really the son of God you'd turn those stones to bread." (Matt. 4:3). We know our Lord was tempted in all points and this must have been the most difficult. That's why Satan always hit him there. God cleared it up for him when his true Father, God, powerfully spoke the same words of all bar mitzvahs, "This is my beloved Son in whom I am well pleased!" This was a pivotal moment of his life. It settled his identity and destiny and launched his ministry. If he needed this powerful blessing, just think how much more we need it.

Mike Singletary was an all-American from Baylor University. He later became a ten-time all-pro with the Chicago Bears and one of the greatest linebackers of all times. He is a member of the Pro Football Hall of Fame, and told me a great story about his son when he worked with our Weekend of Champions programs.

Mike's son came to him upset over kids teasing him about his light skin color.

They taunted, "Are you black or white?"

So he asked his father, "Who am I, Dad?"

Mike marched him into the bathroom and stood him in front of a full-length mirror. Mike asked, "What do you see?"

He answered, "Me!"

Mike continued, "What else?"

He answered, "I see you."

Mike then explained while hugging him from the back, "You see a brave and mighty warrior for God and your father is behind you all the way!"

The air was charged with emotion, and tears ran freely. For years, Mike heard his son often repeat: "I'm a brave and mighty warrior for God and my father is behind me all the way!" No son will ever be the same after he gets this type of powerful blessing from his father.

I told both of my sons this story and their response was, "What a great father." They'd played together at Baylor and were team leaders and friends. Soon after hearing this powerful experience of their old teammate, one of my sons had a chance to use it with his son. One of my grandsons at the time was fourteen years old, and one day after school his dad noticed that his boy seemed discouraged. When his father inquired as to why he was, he explained, "My grades are down, my friends are rejecting me, even the girls who are normally interested aren't. I didn't make the track team, and my world is just caving in."

This was so uncharacteristic for his normally carefree, happy son. His dad knew he needed a big boost to his self-image. His son was having genuine identity problems. He took the young man and marched him to the only full-length mirror in his home and asked, "What do you see?"

He followed Mike's questioning and had the same overwhelming results. When he later told me, we both were weeping unashamedly.

Perhaps this approach is best used in a crisis, but I'm convinced through long personal experience that you don't have to wait for a crisis to arise. All of my children will be able to use this blessing ritual. Since the enemy usually attacks the victim's identity, this powerful visual experience can be a life-changing blessing. Alert parents must be aware enough to see when there is a real challenge to his child's identity and respond strongly.

Having a powerful blessing from my father in my formative years was a source of great strength to me. But it made it terribly hard to go on without him. I felt the void, the emptiness, when he was no longer there to guide and bless me. I was abandoned and utterly alone. At the funeral, a lot of men told me they'd take me fishing and hunting, promising to spend time with me. I waited months, even years, but not one of the guys who had claimed they wanted to see me followed through. It was just talk at the funeral. That just made me miss my father even more and led to real despair. I would visit my father's grave at Seaside Cemetery, hear the roaring surf in the distance and stand there totally alone—feeling abandoned. I felt it so vividly as a boy of fourteen, thinking about those men who said they were going to be a substitute father to me and none did except for my eccentric old uncle. His visits were never really personal but rather just a visit to the house. It was regular enough so that I appreciated it, but after a year, my uncle Weldon moved 500 miles away.

Talk about rejection—it hurts.

When my father died, I felt rejected. I never blamed him, but the results were the same. I needed to regain my sense of identity. I needed a father to stand next to me in a mirror and boldly and loudly proclaim, "You are a mighty warrior for God, brave and strong. Your dad is behind you all the way, and he will go with you to hell and back!"

But my father wasn't there.

A lot of us have been in that situation, and we often deal with it by denial. We tend to say it was no big deal, we really didn't want the job or expect the promotion. Or we say that our families are a mess, that Dad likes my brother best. We deny the hurt. We try to just bull our way through it, stop our whining and get on with life. We insist it won't bother us for long.

We lie to ourselves and others.

But rejection hurts.

"Physical pain and social pain may be more similar than we realize," Matthew Lieberman, a UCLA researcher, said in a news release about a study of thirteen students who played computer games where they were eventually rejected. After several rounds of being ignored and tossed aside by the computer, the students had brain scans. The MRIs revealed physical pain near the right ventral prefrontal cortex. But it happened only after three rounds of computer rejections—once the students were sure it wasn't a technical problem and they were indeed being booted out of the game.

The pain is real.

It's not just being too sensitive. It is a hurt in our heads.

An Akron, Ohio, pastor named Joey Johnson often says, "If your heart is broke, your head don't work right."

The worst part about rejection is we go over and over the situations in our minds. We wish we could say this, explain that. We'd like to take back something we did say. In my case, I kept hearing the promises of those men who said they'd "be there for me," and I was angry when they didn't follow through.

Didn't they know I needed them? Why make a promise they couldn't keep?

Rejection is a deep wound. Sometimes it's bandaged and we are supposed to leave it alone to let it mend. But we tend to pick at it. We rip off the scab and it bleeds again. Soon, it becomes infected. The situation becomes more serious than before. We just want to keep rubbing away the hurt, which now has moved from our heads to our hearts.

That's when my high school coach stepped in. He had been an orphan growing up in the Masonic Home, but he was a great father figure to me. He talked to me in his office, on the football field or in the locker room. Why was the coach so friendly and warm to me? Maybe because he knew we had something in common—no fathers! One of his assistant coaches was Smiley Davis, who had been my father's close friend. He must have briefed Coach Bill Stages. I don't know how it all came about, but I do know Coach Stages spent a lot of time with me. He never said, "I'd like to help fill the hole left when your father died." But I knew that was in his heart. We met just after my dad died. I was still in ninth grade. He came over in the spring to Wynn Seale Junior High and got us all together in the auditorium. It was all the guys wanting to play football. I was a small, clumsy, acne-faced kid. Inside, I was unsure, insecure and heartbroken over what had happened to my father. My father, and especially my brother, had made the Glass name famous in Corpus Christi. My brother was an all-state high school football player, and was then a star at Rice University while I was a third-stringer stumbling around practice. First, I tried quarterback. My brother had been a great quarterback. That was hopeless! Then I became a second-string guard.

But Coach Stages drilled me on all the fundamentals. Despite all my inadequacies, I was an excellent student, a great listener and I wanted to be a player. He seemed to see through all my weaknesses.

"Head up—back flat—eyes wide open—head on a pivot!"

I still hear his words today.

"Stance perfect, relaxed intensity, fire the shoulder and forearm like a flat hunk of steel right into their chop (face and shoulder). Never let them be lower than you. Keep your head up! Fire your body at the ball like a rocket!"

I remember those words, too.

"Stay ahead of the block. Never let them cut you off of your line of pursuit."

And there was more.

"If you make a mistake, make it at full speed!"

Those words, he yelled.

I played for several great coaches in my career, including Blanton Collier and Hall of Famer Paul Brown. But I remembered and applied more from Coach Bill Stages than I did from anyone else. After practice, he always stayed to work extra with me on my technique. It got to be a ritual. He'd often put his hand on my shoulder and walk slowly back to the dressing room with me. He was more than just a coach—he was filling my deep need for blessing.

By my junior year in high school, he had slowly trained this slowest, clumsiest, smallest lineman on the team. Now I was unblockable. In one-on-one drills in practice, I was the best on the team. I had put on fifty pounds and grown four inches to 6-foot-3, 190 pounds. I was lifting weights and getting stronger. He'd meet me at noon in the weight room on my lunch break and train me, just the two of us. Soon other players joined in my private weight-lifting sessions, and the weight room became a popular noontime hang out. At first I resented the other players joining in because I enjoyed the coach's full attention. But he made me the leader of the weight room. In a team meeting he said, "Bill and I have been working out for a long time [actually, just a few weeks] to get stronger. Now we have others joining us. It's not compulsory, but it will help a lot if you want to get stronger."

Few colleges and virtually no high schools had weight programs at that time. Coach Stages often was far ahead of his competition, and this was another example.

But there was more.

I learned how to become highly dominant in the one-on-one drill. Was it to play football better or to please my new coach/dad? I'm now convinced I was seeking his blessing. I was searching for a type of blessing ritual, like the one from my father before I went to bed. Before and after games I sat next to Coach Stages on the team bus. The trip across town took thirty minutes from our dressing room at Ray High School to the City Stadium. It seated 12,000 to 15,000 and was always packed for our games, often with standing room only. Coach Stages talked to the team every morning from 8:15–9:00 A.M. He was an excellent speaker with a great vocabulary. Most of his lectures were about heart and motivation. He wanted us to act in ways that brought honor to our parents, our school and our team. As we sat together on the bus, he'd lecture me in a conversational tone, or sometimes we just sat in silence. Maybe he was too concerned about the game to say much. I vividly remember sitting in his presence with a sense of awe. I respected him! No, it was a form of adoration. I've often wondered why my teammates didn't kid me about our special relationship. He made me a team captain in my senior year. I'm sure if there had been a vote of the players, I never would have won. I was not one of the guys. It was no big deal to be a captain—we had seven—but it meant a lot to me. Coach Stages had chosen me! He did not care if I was struggling with insecurity. He knew I needed this honor.

When I walked to the center of the field for the coin toss or when consulted about a penalty by the officials, I trembled in fear of making the wrong decision. If I had any doubt, I'd always look to the sidelines for his signal. He seemed to know how important it was for me to please him. Once, he pointed back at

me saying, "You make the decision." What a maturing experience that was! I panicked and turned to my best friend, Fred
Morgan, another captain. He made the decision. Naturally, I
agreed. It was a game we had already won and it was relatively
minor. But when Stages pointed back at me, it was like my dad
saying, "I'm with you all the way. Football is no big deal. I'm
with you. Win, lose or draw!"

Coach Stages blessed me in another very special way. My
mother had always called me "William" and insisted that others
do the same.

Coach Stages renamed me!

"You are Bill, not William!" he said. "I don't want a 'Sweet
William,' What I want is a rough, tough Bill."

I always thought he insisted on the name change because he
wanted me to have his name.

What a blessing!

But my father's blessing also stayed with me after his death,

He had often assured me that I was the "apple of his eye,"
regardless of what happened to me on the football field. He
knew I was hurting. I had grown up in the shadow of my super-
brother. My early junior high sports efforts were terrible, and I
was the younger brother of the best-known high school player in
the sports-crazed town of Corpus Christi. People felt sorry for
me because I wasn't living up to the Glass name athletically. Dad
seemed to know how I felt and would say just the right thing to
encourage me.

We all need those encouraging words, and we all can hear the blessing from someone even after that person is gone from our lives—just like we all can remember the curses and criticism we received from people who have been dead for years. Everyone has a deep craving for the security and the identity of parental blessing. It's at the core of all of us.

I long assumed that everyone had a father like mine, someone who loved to bless his children. But as I grew older and talked to more men about this, I realized that I was blessed to have a father who blessed me. I have a close friend who told me of his tortured journey to connect with his own father. His dad continually withheld the blessing. Making it even more painful, my friend's father would bless the younger son. My friend is a good man who worked so hard to earn that blessing. It never came, and there was even more agony after his father's death. He was cut out of the will, while his brother was given one last blessing of the entire estate. Like Esau, he lost his birthright and blessing, creating a pain that led to a hole in his heart that he still longs to fill.

If a person doesn't find it in a healthy way, he can self-destruct in the search for a blessing. Criminals kill for the security of the gang. The gang fills all of their basic "blessing" needs. The gang takes the place of their father. It gives them an identity when they stick a gun or a knife in your face. They have immediate significance.

It may be false, but it seems real to them.

It meets the same need I had running the hot towels to my dying dad. The gang fills the same need I had for love and connection with someone important. If it is not as God intended, a strong father on earth and in heaven, the need is so basic that it must be filled by even the Crips, the Bloods and other gangs. The gang has a leader. Gang members call each other brothers and sisters. They give the illusion of a family, a place to go, a group of people who accept you for who are. They have your back. They make you think they are blessing you, accepting you, protecting you.

We all want those things. We need those things. It's a deep yearning, vital to our well-being. We will find it in one place or another, good or bad. Parents should be the ones who meet this need, who deliver the blessing, who give children a sense of connection and belonging. My father and coaches did it. For some of us, there was a special teacher, a grandmother, someone besides our parents who blessed us, and they are responsible for much of who we are today. We must do that for our children.

PERSONAL APPLICATION AND PRAYER

✝ My dad's unconditional love had nothing to do with my performance, good or bad.

✝ My dad's death caused a loss of identity in my young life.

✝ Christ could not have a bar mitzvah at age thirteen like the normal Jewish boy because only the father could conduct a bar mitzvah for his own children.

✝ Since Christ had no earthly father, he had to wait for his bar mitzvah until age thirty at his baptism. He performed no miracles and preached no sermons and did little of importance until he received his Heavenly Father's bar mitzvah blessing. It was pivotal in the life of Christ.

✝ If blessing was that much of a watershed in the life of our Lord, how much more is it a must for all of us?

✝ It was to me a craving! It is to you and your children and their children also.

✝ Every child has an identity crisis when they ask, "Who am I?" If they have a father like Mike Singletary who explains, "You are a mighty warrior for God, strong and brave. Your father is behind you all the way," they are blessed.

PRAYER

*Oh God, keep me alert to look for
the identity crisis and help me to skillfully act
quickly to be powerfully there "behind them all
the way" with your empowering presence
through me. For Christ's sake, Amen!*

Chapter Eight

WE ALL NEED A
SPIRITUAL FATHER

I have a spiritual father.

I need a spiritual father, one with skin on, a heart that beats, a person in the same room with me. I'm not ashamed to admit this. I know some of you feel the same way, but you tell yourself that you're an adult. Perhaps you are even a parent or a grandparent. If anything, you should be a spiritual parent to someone else—not need one yourself.

Well, it works both ways.

We can be biological parents and grandparents.

We also can be spiritual parents and grandparents.

But guess what? We need help, too. I give you permission to seek out a spiritual father, one with skin on and a heart who longs to bless and nurture you. Some of us need to realize that our parents may never bless us. They are emotionally incapable or just too stubborn to do it. We can spend the rest of our lives longing for a blessing we'll never receive from someone who has no interest in giving it. Some parents don't get it, won't get it or can't get it.

We need to accept that.

Then we need to remember Psalm 68:5: "A father to the fatherless, a defender of widows is God in his holy dwelling."

How does God do this?

Psalm 68:6: "God sets the lonely in families."

Think about that promise for a moment—God is speaking through a prayer written by King David.

God sets the lonely in families.

Spiritual families.

Better families.

My father died when I was fourteen. Maybe your father died when you were young. Maybe he lived, but was absent in spirit. Maybe he never deserved to be called a father and never will. Maybe you need a Psalm 68 spiritual family if your biological family is gone or just not able to be the spiritual guide that you need. If you're a man, it's best to have a spiritual father. It is not a sign of weakness—it's an indication of wisdom. There's a reason Jesus sent out the disciples in pairs. There's a reason Jesus put together a dozen friends, known as the apostles, and became a spiritual father to them. There's also a reason Jesus often left his friends behind to pray—he was connecting with God the Father, who happens to be the spiritual father of Jesus. Read about it in Matthew 26:36–45. It's the night before his death. He knows what is coming. He asks his two best friends—Peter and John—to pray with him, as Jesus goes to his spiritual father for strength. Peter and John can't stay awake. Jesus ends up in a heart-to-heart, and, yes, a heartbreaking conversation with God the Father as he learns his prayers won't be answered, that the pain and humiliation and betrayals to come must be faced.

He needed the blessing of his father to do it.

Sometimes, that's a father's message. It's not changing a situation. It's not so much giving advice. It's simply saying, "I know you are strong enough to handle this. I'm behind you. I am with you." That is the essence of the message Jesus heard from God the Father. It's something we sometimes need to be told.

Think about it—if Jesus needed a spiritual father, what makes us any different?

I have a spiritual father. To me, he's a man of towering intellect. A man of great wisdom and depth. He recently was in my office and said, "Bill, I heard your taped message on the blessing and I really liked it!"

I said, "Thank you, sir. But did you know I was talking about you when I was talking about my spiritual father?"

He said, "Sure."

I asked, "How did you know? I didn't mention your name."

He shrugged, "You described your father as a man of towering intellect, deeply spiritual, with great wisdom, who is in his eighties. Who else do you know who has great intellect, is a man of wisdom who's in his eighties and blesses you?"

We named the office building of our ministry for Fred Smith, my mentor, my father figure, my friend. Our relationship began when I was in college. As a sophomore, I was chairman of Campus Focus Week at Baylor. Christian businessmen and other leaders spoke to classes, chapel services and at nightly rallies. I met Fred that week and spoke to him several times. I took notes from the things he said. Fifty years later, I still take notes from the things Fred tells me. Before retiring, Fred was a management consultant for several major companies. He also was a well-known speaker and served on the board of *Christianity Today*, along with writing for *Leadership Magazine*. He recently wrote a book entitled *Leadership with Integrity*. It's a fantastic book. Get it and read it. It will help you understand why it means so much to me when Fred blesses me, whether on the phone or in person. Even when he agrees with me totally, I still need his reinforcement and encouragement. One of the major ways Fred blesses me is by his interest and concern. I can't overstate his support when we went through a major crisis in our ministry. He was there in every way—not only there physically, but also by calling mutual friends and suggesting they might want to encourage me. Fred gives me great advice, and he remains positive, but he also points out other ways of thinking that are helpful. He's kind enough to point out weaknesses and helps me work on them. He usually does it in a nonthreatening way, telling a story of someone else who failed or succeeded in a similar situation, pointing out that I should be careful in these same areas.

It's a super strategy.

Fred often blesses me with a few words.

He tells me, "You're real."

He tells me, "You're genuine."

He sometimes tells me, "You don't have pretense like some other Christian leaders. There's not a phony bone in your body."

How often I need to hear something like that.

The blessing must be honest, not manipulative. Never maneuver someone with a blessing. Be direct and be believable!

That's the key to picking a spiritual father. He doesn't have to be perfect. He doesn't even have to be right all the time, but he should have a pretty good batting average when it comes to advice. Most of all, he has to be worthy of your trust. He has to be without a personal agenda when dealing with you and capable of seeing your best qualities and reminding you of them—especially when you need a lift.

If you want a real spiritual father, then you must understand there will be times when that person will not tell you what you want to hear. And the key to being the right kind of spiritual father is to have the guts to tell the person what they need to hear —do it in love, but still do it, even if you know it will hurt. Better to cause some pain now than long-term agony later.

Where did Fred learn to bless people like me?

A spiritual father for him was Maxey Jarman, founder and CEO of Genesco Corporation. Jarman pronounced "the blessing" on Fred Smith when he introduced him to a business associate: "He's got one of the five best minds I've ever met," Jarman said.

On a train trip to buy a company, Jarman told Fred, "Your lack of education won't stand in the way of your advancement in this company. You have an excellent mind and tremendous potential."

At the time, Maxey Jarman's shoe company was at its peak, so everything he said to Fred was gospel when it came to business. Most people in the company were college graduates; Fred wasn't. Inspired by Jarman's confidence, Fred read constantly to make up for his lack of formal education. He has since lectured at many universities, though he never attended college, and has received two honorary doctorates. He has the best mind that I've ever met, an amazing mix of spirituality and pure intellect.

Recently I was thanking him for being such a great mentor to me, and he quickly said, "A mentor needs someone to mentor. You filled a need for me because you were always so eager to learn."

Now, I think of my three fathers. My biological father has been dead for more than fifty years, but then I had a wonderful father figure in my high school football coach. Then came my spiritual father, Fred Smith, who is now eighty-nine. He is physically deteriorating. As I visit Fred, I'm reliving my dad's slow and painful death. Fred has battled failing kidneys and has been on dialysis for several years. He's often close to death, but then he rallies! I feel selfish because I can't help but feel alone, as I was when my first father died. I keep repeating, "He can't die! He must live! There is no one who could possibly take his place. What can I do? Would hot towels help?"

But in the end, the hot towels that I brought my father couldn't keep him away from death's door, and the same is true with Fred Smith. I've even offered one of my kidneys. He refused as he often does with a joke, "You have to go to the bathroom constantly. Your kidneys are worse than mine."

I was serious; he wasn't.

Finally, he explained that the doctors assured him that a kidney transplant is impossible in his case, and he said he thought it was unethical for him to take a kidney at his age when so many younger people are in need of one. That has inspired me to make sure that my organs are donated to someone who needs them when I die. Sometimes I feel empty. I can't help him, just like I couldn't help my father. I pray for him daily. There are days I think about him constantly. The new blessing in all this pain is that I often visit him at his home or at the dialysis center where he has his blood cleaned for four hours every other day. What a privilege to have his undivided attention for those four hours. Major corporations once paid him huge sums of money for his advice. I've had it free for almost fifty years. But it was more than advice that he gave me. It was his blessing! Yes, even with his body failing, he still blesses me. His mind is strong, his reasoning clear. He avoids discussions of his health, simply saying he feels "regular," meaning not much has changed, and the situation is not very good.

When he first found out about having to be on dialysis for the rest of his life, he gave me a book called *Tuesdays with Morrie*. Morrie was an old college professor of the author Mitch Albom. He was dying from ALS (amyotrophic laterial sclerosis). Mitch flew from Detroit to Boston every week on Tuesday to meet with his beloved old teacher. They sat and talked.

Like Fred, his body was failing, but his mind was sharp to the end. Fred never told me why he gave me the book. He just gave it to me with body language and verbal hints to not get "syrupy about it." Fred is turned off by over-the-top emotions; his word for it is "syrupy."

But he was obviously saying to me, "This is me and you."

As I read the detailed story of the visits and the inspirational relationship of student and professor, I realized it was actually a father/son story. Morrie was dying physically, but was pouring his last wisdom into his student. Morrie remains a teacher to the end, and Mitch remains a student. It became increasingly diffi-cult for me to read the moment-by-moment account of Tuesdays with Morrie because it was too similar to my Tuesdays with Fred at the dialysis center.

There were days I found it almost impossible to read through the tears. But I never let Fred see me cry because he'd grunt, "No syrupiness!"

Fred once told me, "How often do you get a call from a friend without a purpose? Usually they want advice or something! I don't know of anyone who calls just to have a connection with me and just because they care about me! Even if they do, they cover up with a reason for the call."

At the time, I let it pass without comment. But it kept eating at me. The next day I dropped by to see him face-to-face.

I said, "Fred, I call often just because I care."

I had tears in my eyes.

He said, "You're different. You're family. You belong."

That's a blessing we all need to hear.

One day as I was writing this book, I had some doubts. Maybe I was overemphasizing the blessing. But later I drove down the street and saw a beautiful Mercedes Benz. Slumped behind the wheel was my neighbor, John. He's a big, powerful businessman, his wife a fine attorney. He's a success in every way—a good Christian, good father and good husband. Yet there is something missing.

I decided to scratch a little.

"Tell me about your dad," I said.

He cleared his throat and looked away. I realized he was struggling with his cool shades to wipe away the tears. He was obviously not comfortable crying in front of me.

He said his siblings had often asked how he handled his father's anger, because he was often singled out. His father cursed him. John became a driven man, an overachiever in search of a blessing.

Then he said something that shocked me, "I'd like you to be my substitute father."

I was honored to bless him, just as Fred Smith does me.

If you look for it, you may get that chance, too.

How do you find a spiritual father? Or if you are a woman, a spiritual mother?

You ask.

First, in prayer.

Tell God that you need someone to bless you, to guide you, to speak into your life with no agenda other than love. Ask God if there already is a person like that in your life. If not, ask God to send you one. Then have the courage to ask someone to do it. Explain the role of a spiritual parent. Maybe even show them this book. You may think you'll be rejected, especially if you've been battling rejection much of your life. But if you've first gone to God, then maybe to a friend or perhaps a pastor, God will begin to speak through someone. And don't be surprise if the person agrees to do it. Most of us would be honored to fill that role in a younger person's life.

PERSONAL APPLICATION AND PRAYER

✝ Our Heavenly Father is of eternal importance. But we also need a spiritual father—one with skin on. He always has lasting influence for the rest of our lives and even points us toward God, the ultimate Father. There is an obvious connection between these two fathers.

✝ I give Fred Smith credit for helping me make all of the important decisions in my life and ministry. He once responded to my praise by saying, "There were one or two decisions that you made without my advice and I sure don't want credit for those." He was right. I hadn't asked his advice, and our organization briefly floundered because of it. He did step in with wise counsel during this crisis.

✝ On another occasion, I was thanking Fred for his wise suggestions and his typical humble response was, "The teacher arrives when the student is ready. A mentor needs someone to mentor. You fill a need for me also. You have always been so anxious to learn."

✝ Fred makes me feel loved, valued and that I belong. Fred once said to me, "You are family," and I felt "belonging." This was difficult for him to say because he was always basically repulsed by "syrupiness" (that's what he calls overly emotional subjects). I sensed that he was even uncomfortable in saying, "You're family." It slipped out and was quickly covered by an abrupt change of subject. He usually broke the overly serious subjects with humor. But his humor always had a point. Later, I'd ask myself, "Did he have a deeper point to make?" The answer was —Yes!

PRAYER

Thank you, God, for Fred Smith.

What a great spiritual father he's been to me!

Father, I pray you lead everyone reading

this to a spiritual father or mother.

Thank you, Lord, for his blessing and advice.

For Christ's sake, Amen.

Chapter Nine

BE A FATHER, NOT A COACH

Our society loves coaches. They are sometimes called generals, empire builders, czars and geniuses. They are stars, often bigger and more well-known than their players. The cameras sometimes spend more time on them than the game and athletes. They make commercials. They can earn as much as $25,000 to give a single motivational speech for a corporation. They write books. They may even run for political office.

They may be great leaders, but they can be lousy fathers.

Remember that: You can be a great leader, a super coach—and a lousy father.

Rarely does a coach bless his players. His love is conditional, based on performance. He may talk about his team being a family, but if a player doesn't perform to expectations, he is traded or cut. If he's seriously injured, he's forced into retirement.

Winning is the bottom line at the pro, top college levels and sometimes even in high school.

If there is a true relationship between players and coaches, it is often one of convenience that works for both parties. But not in a family. A true family has a relationship based on a covenant, just as God has with us. The Lord says, "I will never leave you or forsake you." You can read about that in Hebrews 13:1–6 or Joshua 1:5–11.

Coaches can't afford to say that. They can't risk their job on playing a slumping quarterback whose confidence is shaken, not if they lose more than a few games with the guy. Then the pressure builds to bench him and play someone else. The coach will have to forsake the quarterback. That's sports. That's how it's supposed to be—the best should play. If the coach doesn't win, his team loses money. Attendance drops, critics scream, fans grumble and the coach is fired. Families are not run like this, or at least they aren't if they are following God's model.

But so often, we act more like coaches and less like fathers.

I was recently speaking about this in a distant state when a state senator laid his head on my shoulder and cried until my jacket was wet with his tears.

I said, "Senator, what in the world's wrong with you?"

He said, "I've got five grown sons; every one of them hates my guts."

I said, "Why do they hate you, Senator?"

He said, "I always keep the blessing just out of reach. I'm always saying, if only you'd have done this it would have been better . . ."

I've played for some football coaches like that.

They'd growl, "You did a good job, but if only you'd have done this . . ."

You may argue, "At least he said you did a good job!"

But if you follow it by saying, "If only you'd have done this it would have been better," that's no blessing.

That's saying you really didn't make it. That's keeping the blessing frustratingly just out of reach. That's typical of many coaches, but it really stinks for fathers.

Have you ever had a job evaluation?

Your boss may have started out by telling you all the things that you're doing right, and why you are a valued employee, but . . .

Yes, that "BUT . . ."

The moment you hear the "BUT," you know the bad stuff is coming. You know the blessing is being jerked away. You know this is really about business.

There is a scene from the movie *North Dallas Forty* where a pro football player argues with a coach.

The player says, "Every time I say this is a business, you tell me it's a sport. When I say it's a sport, you say it's a business."

Which is it? Whatever works best for the coach at any given moment.

That's life in the cutthroat world of business or pro sports.

But it can destroy families.

My father was able to be a dad first. He'd take me fishing and tried to teach me how to fish right. But if I fouled up and made too much noise, got a backlash in my reel (which I did often), failed to get the bait on the hook properly, hit the side of the boat scaring the fish away or failed to spit on the bait (he always did) . . . well, he didn't care. He'd say, "Catching fish isn't important—it's just fishing with you that counts."

He decided what counts.

I finally figured it out. He made it so abundantly clear by the way he draped his big loving arms and hands around me, touching me in a hug or on my head or face. He knew fishing was about us being together, not competing. Football was king in my hometown of Corpus Christi, and in our family, sports of all kinds were overemphasized. But in fishing, hunting, playing catch in the front yard and other activities, the rules and traditions went out the window when compared to his love and blessing of me. Football was great, but not that important. "If you never play a down, I'll always love you just as much. You don't have to get a scholarship for football like your brother. I've got plenty of money. "

He'd say things like, "If you're going to catch fish, you can't kick the side of the boat and talk loud. But I only care about *you*—it's not that important to catch fish!"

The message was clear: Fishing is fun, but *you* are what counts. Football is great, but *you* are what counts. Even before his life was cut short by Hodgkin's disease, he focused on the blessing. It was as if he sensed he would not live long and had to pack all the blessings and encouragement he could into his family. Once he knew his days were numbered, his blessing became more frequent and intense.

His only complaint was, "I just wish I could watch Vernon [my older brother] play his senior year at Rice." He did live long enough to see Vernon named preseason all-American quarterback, but he died in May before Vernon's senior year began the following September.

He was so different than most coaches, the exception being my high school coach, Bill Stages. My other coaches all had a thinly hidden desire to win and only a secondary love for the players. That's all right and to be expected of coaches, but it's destructive for fathers. Players who are out of favor are much more likely to be verbally abused than those who are at the top of their game. I never heard Jim Brown criticized by coaches. His mistakes on and off the field were covered up by coaches and owners. I even noticed that my mistakes were ignored when I played a great game otherwise. Assistant coaches never criticized superstars. Head coaches did it carefully. I was talking recently to a head coach who played when I did, and he deplored how things had changed. He said, "It would never happen in our day. Recently, I had a player who told me in no uncertain terms that he was paid four times what I am and he could get me fired—I knew his threats were true."

I played for Paul Brown, Hall of Famer and one of the greatest coaches in National Football League history. He is credited with being the first pro coach to have players keep notebooks, watch films and do extensive pregame preparation. He is believed to be the first coach to put assistants in the press box and talk to them on headphones so he could find out what they observed from high above the field. Often, it's very difficult to have a true picture of the game from ground level because the action is so quick, bodies get in your way and you can't see what's happening across the field. Sometimes coaches say "I need to watch the film" to avoid answering a reporter's question that they didn't like. But on other occasions, they really do need to look at the game films to truly understand what happened on a key play.

Because of Paul Brown and the success he had coaching the Browns in the 1950s and 1960s, virtually every pro and college team began using game films and coaches in the press box. Then it spread to the high schools and lower levels.

As a football coach in his era, Paul Brown was an innovator and a football genius.

But he had zero interest in blessing his players.

He motivated by making greater and unrealistic demands, and sometimes, through fear. His goal was a perfect game. No one is perfect, and Brown knew that. But he also believed the closer his teams came to playing that perfect game, the more they'd win. And he was right.

My coauthor, Terry Pluto, wrote a book on the World Champion 1964 Cleveland Browns called *Browns Town, 1964*. He discovered that more than thirty years after playing for Paul Brown, many of the players still recalled his words—his sometimes sarcastic, cutting, cryptic comments.

Linebacker Galen Fiss remembered Brown telling him, "Galen, we can't do it for you."

Defensive back Bernie Parrish was scorched when Brown said, "Bernie, don't tell me the great ones do it that way."

Hall of Famer Lou Groza still felt uneasy when he thought of Brown's words, "Lou, you are killing our football team."

A player named Junior Wren never forgot Brown telling him, "I've seen better performances from high school players."

For defensive lineman Paul Wiggin, it was a game where his roughing the kicker penalty turned a 17–14 victory for the Browns into a 21–17 loss. That happened on a Sunday. Brown always gave his players Monday and Tuesday off. Wiggin said, "I didn't sleep for three nights . . . I was so scared about what he'd say."

Wednesday came, Brown showed the film of Wiggin's penalty just once and then told the entire team, "Gentlemen, if we are not in the championship game December 27, we'll know to thank."

Curiously, Wiggin was not a starter at the time of the penalty, but Brown put him in the lineup the following Sunday. He had three sacks, the Browns won and Wiggin was awarded a game ball. When everyone else had left the dressing room, Brown approached Wiggin and simply said, "Hey, Wig, thanks."

That may be great motivation for coaches, but a father can destroy his children with those same threats and scare tactics.

Every player lived in fear of hearing Brown say, "Turn in your suit."

That meant hand in your uniform, you were cut.

It was more than thirty years later, and these men still felt the sting of Paul Brown's words! Most had become very successful in their careers after football. We are all part of the 1964 Browns team that won the title, a team that was coached by Blanton Collier, who took over after Paul Brown was fired.

Yet part of Paul Brown was branded on our brains.

There have been many coaches like Paul Brown, and some coaches still have a little of that personality in them. Fear can be a terrific motivator, at least in the short term. But it can kill families.

Yes, children need discipline, but even more, they need to have dreams and goals.

Fathers are pivotal in those areas.

But few fathers bless, and even fewer know how to be a real father. They find it much more comfortable to coach. Perhaps it's because their fathers were more like coaches, or they had a coach who was the closest thing they had to a father figure.

Many of us who played for strong coaches such as Paul Brown are conflicted. We respect their knowledge, their intelligence and how they helped mold us into winners. But there is a part of us that feels uneasy, a part that may still be wounded by some of those things said and done to us by those coaches.

It should not be that way with our parents.

How many of us are adults, but still feel like we need to measure up to the expectations of our parents? They may be senior citizens. They may be dead. They may not want anything from us except an occasional call or visit.

But we feel like they want more.

How much more? More of what? We can't even answer the questions, but we just feel like we didn't do enough   at least in their eyes.

It goes back to the coaching mentality.

The Minnesota Vikings rate their players on a scale with 2.0 being the perfect score. Players receive marks like 1.2, 1.5, even a 1.9. But no one ever gets the 2.0.

That's because no one ever plays a perfect game, at least in the eyes of the coaches. They'll tell players, "You were really good out there, but it would have been better if you had . . ."

When the coach says, "You did a good job, but if only you'd done this it would have been better," he's saying you didn't make it. The players are presented with their scores. They watch the film with their coaches, seeing all the good plays and mistakes. Most of the time is spent on the mistakes or the area that needs to be improved. In football, they tell you the films don't lie. No matter how well you think you played, how savvy a certain move was or how you think you had a great game, the films reveal a different story.

I once had a coach show the film of me missing a tackle. The entire team was watching it. The coach yelled, "Just a minute, stop the film. Let's run it back. Let's see if Bill makes the tackle this time."

Of course, I didn't.

Same play, same mistake.

The coach said, "Let's try it one more time, run it back. Maybe Bill will make the play."

I missed again.

That's all he did, run it back and reshow it a few times. He made his point. I vowed never to mess up that kind of play again. Coaches expect excellence, and players are seldom extravagantly praised. Players are told their errors won't be tolerated, and coaches use every tactic imaginable to get the message across. They will intimidate, humiliate, repudiate. They will bring up anything to make the player feel guilty.

They say things like, "The team was expecting better than that. You let us down."

How many of us have heard lines like that from our own parents? How many of us were told about how we have disappointed the family, how we are bringing embarrassment to our parents? Or how they have given us so much, and we are giving back so little?

How many of us remember our parents saying, "If only you had done . . . this or that."

How many of us felt inadequate when hearing that, yet find ourselves saying the same things to our own children?

How many of us don't say these things, but just scowl or roll our eyes in disgust?

How many of us have done this to our own children—the

words coming from our mouths even as we remember how we swore we'd never say those things to our own children because they had hurt us so much?

Coaching our kids is not a good idea. The *if onlys* may work for coaches, but they stink for parents. And we need parents who bless us rather than parents who act like coaches and give us mixed blessings. Because I played in the NFL for a dozen years, I receive the league's alumni magazine. They featured a survey of the last 1,000 players to retire, and it revealed that 800 of them were broke, jobless or divorced within five years after leaving football. These problems aren't indications that these men are losers, but it does suggest that athletic success doesn't always equal personal success. Being an athlete isn't the same as being a real man or husband and father. The discipline can be good for you. The relationships can last a lifetime. There are many tremendous lessons to be learned from coaches and sports.

But there is a better way to be a parent.

PERSONAL APPLICATION AND PRAYER

✝ Coaches are prone to say, "You did a good job, but if only you would have done this . . . it would have been better!" That's saying you didn't make it—you didn't measure up. That isn't a blessing. It's okay and to be expected from the coach, but it isn't the role of the father.

✝ My dad understood blessing. He'd say, "Fishing is fun, but *you* are what counts. If you hit the side of the boat it may scare the fish away, but I really only care about you."

✝ My dad had the same blessing attitude about sports. He would say, "If you get a football scholarship like your older brother, good. If you don't, I'll pay your way gladly. Football isn't that important anyway. You'll probably make your mark in another far more important profession."

✝ I played for a demanding, negative, verbally abusive coach like Paul Brown. He made us fear and respect him. John Grisham's book *Bleachers* featured a coach who was summed up by one of his star players with this potent line, "We couldn't decide whether we hated him or loved him, but he did make us win."

✝ The good father can't cast these kinds of shadows of doubt. His blessing is pivotal. Discipline is a part of blessing. But his one great purpose is an unconditional blessing. It should be clearly and creatively delivered.

PRAYER

God, forgive me for trying to coach my children. Help me to catch them doing something right so I can bless them! For Christ's sake, Amen.

Chapter Ten

AVOID MIXED MESSAGES

Here are my rules:

If you are going to bless, then bless.

If you are going to discipline, then discipline.

If you are not sure whether to bless or discipline, then bless.

Whatever you do, don't mix your discipline and blessing. "No mixed messages" is the most important rule in this area. Blessings should be regular, at least daily. A parent should bless each child before bed. It should be nothing but love, nothing but positive reinforcement, nothing that would ever make the child doubt they belong to you and will always belong to you.

It's not a time to talk about what they did wrong.

I tried to discipline my kids in creative ways. And parents, this is just from my experience. You can find your own ways of discipline. When driving on a long trip to California, the boys were fighting in the backseat of our station wagon. I drove onto an empty service road in the middle of the desert. I made them get out and run. They chased our car down the service road for a while in 105-degree heat. When I figured they'd had enough, I let them crawl through the rear window and fall into a puddle of their own sweat in the back end of the station wagon. I made sure they had plenty of water. We had no problem with fights for a while after that, and the noise level inside the car subsided drastically. I did this on a couple of occasions during that trip because it was necessary to maintain some semblance of peace in the car. After that, only the threat of more running was enough.

But when I blessed them that night, I did not say, "I love you, you're mine and I think you're terrific. But I'd love you even more if you'd be quiet in the back of the car."

Nothing could change my love for them.

Remember, don't mix blessing with discipline.

Know why?

In most cases, discipline really tells the child, "Here's how you didn't quite measure up."

How did I handle the kids in the car?

I said, "Acting up doesn't make me love you any less, but we'd all have more fun if you guys could cut down the noise."

Boys have a lot of aggressive energy, and it needs to be released. That's why I decided to make them run. They also wanted to be athletes, and I told them, "Great athletes can run in the heat." Obviously, I didn't let them run too long because that could be dangerous. Common sense has to overrule anger.

When I was playing with the Browns, I went to preach in a church. My sons were in Sunday school, and after the service, a lady approached me, laughing. She said the children had been asked how their parents disciplined them.

"Your sons said you kicked them," she said. "Now I'm sure that it's not true, but I knew you'd find it humorous."

I said, "They're exactly right. I do kick them. I don't kick them as in a kickoff. I just give them a little punt as in a fourth down situation. I don't lift them off of the ground. It certainly couldn't be considered abusive. A small kick in the butt with the side of my foot is good for them."

She was confused, to say the least.

The reason I resorted to the punt is because my hands were so sore and bruised from playing defensive end and jamming them into big offensive tackles. It would hurt me more than them to use my hands. An occasional punt in the rear did wonders to get their attention. Proverbs 13:22 says, "A good man leaves an inheritance for his children's children."

An inheritance of blessing should include discipline and love. Discipline is a part of love. When you don't discipline, it indicates that you don't care enough to make them behave. But it must be started very young, while they are open and responsive. If you wait until they are in teen rebellion, it's too late. Mavis was always alert to any sign of any wrong direction they may be taking. She is a great mom—loving and blessing, but also difficult to con. We must have been a good combination because they are such well-adjusted individuals. Our three children aren't perfect, but they are high-achieving Christian parents and leaders.

I know the Bible says that to spare the rod is to spoil the child, but if we continually resort to spanking, it lessens the impact. As a child, I was spanked only once, but I was disciplined often. My parents knew they couldn't let me get away with bad behavior. Use creative consequences to get their attention. You can make them run, do push-ups or perform some extra chores. But don't do it to be cruel. Don't make an immediate decision about a major punishment when you are angry. Cool down and think about it. Don't verbally attack them. Don't call them demeaning names.

Ephesians 4:26 reads: "Do not let the sun go down on you while you are still angry."

I really did take this to heart. I made sure there wasn't any anger or bitterness left in their hearts before we slept. If I had overreacted and yelled at them, I asked forgiveness. I always expressed my love in some way.

I remember telling them, "You know I love you and I just can't allow you to ruin the trip for the rest of us. You are terrific, but real winners like you are always considerate of others. You are team players and you want the team to win. We can't win if everybody can't get along and have fun."

I always gave them a hug, and I always kissed them on the mouth or cheek. This transition from discipline to blessing is imperative. Because the atmosphere of love and belonging must dominate the relationship. The message is: You are a treasure that I prize and value. If it isn't always stated, it is still the overpowering idea beneath all that is said. When in doubt, always say it.

Good parenting is stating and restating the obvious. Love, value and belonging are pivotal. Christian values are always reinforced in a positive way. Don't say "I love you" unless it's genuine. But if you really mean it, then say it a lot. Most of all, no matter what has happened, never withhold your love or the blessing. If you keep the blessing just out of reach, you build a prison cell for your child. If not an actual one, then a psychological one. There are so many overachievers in our country, people whose parents couldn't just say, "Good job, you're mine and I'll always love you."

They had to do a little coaching and teaching, even when they thought they were doing something loving to their children. Love has to be unconditional or it's not love—it's negotiation. The two must be kept totally separate.

A blessing can involve performance-based statements: "Great catch. . . . Great hit. . . . You are so honest!"

Just don't add *if only* or *but* after it.

Concentrate on reinforcing good character traits. Be specific. Say things like, "I was really proud of you when you asked your brother's forgiveness for borrowing his shirt without permission."

This kind of blessing shows you are paying attention to what is happening in the lives of your children. My father's greatest blessing to me was telling me, "If you don't want to play football, baseball or any sport, I'll pay for your college."

He said this even though my brother had gone to Rice on a football scholarship and was predicted to be an all-American quarterback for Rice. My dad was searching for ways to reassure me of his love and blessing, which had nothing to do with my performance. He knew it was hard to be in my brother's intimidating athletic shadow.

He'd assure me, "You'll make your mark in this world in other and maybe even more important ways than your brother."

Because of this, I felt no jealousy toward my brother. He was seven years older and my hero. I loved being his little brother, even though I was inferior athletically. When people would compare us, it made me feel as if I was put down. But it didn't bother me for long. I heard my father's blessings in my head, and that fought off those feelings of inferiority. He blessed me and I believed it!

I believed it because he blessed me each night, and because I knew he believed what he was saying. I still hear his words, "I'm with you all the way to hell and back." Even when I was too young to really understand what that meant, I still knew my father loved and supported me. His phrase "to hell and back" made me know he was with me always and through anything I may face.

And I did have trials, like most kids.

Sometimes people would ask, "Why aren't you a great athlete like your brother?"

When my father was present, he'd immediately come to my defense. I didn't mind anyone trying to put me down because I knew he was there, and I felt blessed just hearing him support me.

He never discussed sex with me except to show great love and respect for my mother, whom he adored. I was allowed total freedom around him, but even the slightest disrespect of my mother brought a swift reaction. She was the queen of the house and could never be treated any less than a queen. Dishonesty was not allowed. "Tell me the truth regardless. I'll always be on your side, but never lie. Nothing is worse than a sniveling thief! Never steal!"

He hated gossip: "If you can't say something nice, don't say anything at all. I will not tolerate it. I don't want to hear it. It's being little to talk about someone. Don't lower yourself to do it."

He taught me cleanliness and manners, "how to treat a woman," table manners, even bathroom manners (how to urinate and not be heard, since you never know if a woman may be in the next room). You must not let her hear you going to the bathroom—that's bad manners. Not as bad as sin, but close.

He always praised his wife's cooking. He knew it was a real insult to show any type of disdain for what your mother puts on the table. He would not tolerate anyone criticizing his wife, and he certainly wouldn't let us say anything bad about our mother. If you wanted to get my father angry, just do anything that even hinted at disrespect for her. He used the terms "your mother . . . my wife." It was a sign of respect, and he made it clear we didn't dare violate the rules of the house.

Table manners were important: Keep your mouth closed when you chew, take small bites, eat slower, don't smack your lips. To him, a man without manners was "low class."

Cussing was tolerated if you didn't use the Lord's name in vain, but never use swear words of any kind around women. They must be respected. He was never neutral or silent about anything moral. He made his convictions clear. The Bible was his guide, but there were also a lot of east Texas and family traditions thrown in, almost equal to scripture. He would never admit it, but it was true.

He hated racial prejudice and told a lot of stories in which minorities did the right thing and "white trash" were the villains. He was a liberal politically. He loved FDR and was proud to pay taxes to our great country. He loved being an American and bragged about the country. The fact that a lot of his friends disagreed about paying taxes didn't bother him. He knew what he believed. Had he lived today, it's possible his politics would be different. But he would never change what he believed just to fit in or please someone else.

Watching his life taught me more than any words of wisdom he may have given me. That's why I believe teaching must be kept to a minimum.

Why?

Because they already know what you believe even before you say it. They watch you so carefully and listen to you so thoroughly that they know exactly "where you stand" on every issue. My sons and daughter can anticipate what I'm going to say down to the word because they have listened to me, heard my messages and been around me so much. For me to try to constantly teach them is usually counterproductive. I continue to fall into the same trap everyone else does, but the ideal would be to try not to lecture that much.

When I did discipline or teach my children, I made a point to explain that I was unhappy with their action, with what they did   not who they are in my eyes or the eyes of God.

I'd tell them, "You know, if I didn't love you I would allow you to act up, but since I love you, I must discipline you. "

Proverbs 13:24 reads: "He who spares the rod hates the child, but he who loves the child is careful to discipline them."

The key word is "careful." I really think my children believed I was careful in how and when I disciplined them because I blessed them regularly and unconditionally. Before they spank children, some parents say, "This is going to hurt me more than it does you." But then the parent tells the child what a lousy person they are and how they will never amount to anything as they whack their behinds.

What do you think that child really learned from the spanking?

That their own parent doesn't think they're worth much. That they deserve to be beaten is something they take personally. It's the worst kind of discipline: The problem becomes *who* they are, not *what* they did. Children continually disciplined in this way grow up resenting their parents and having doubts about themselves. When my children were young, I was careful to discipline the bad behavior and bless the person.

"You are such a fantastic person that I can't allow you to act that way . . . a great guy like you doesn't do that type of thing," I'd say.

Once they became teenagers and began to rebel, I backed away. I don't think you can teach a teenager a great deal during the rebellion period. When they know what you want, they want the opposite.

You love the Bible, they don't like the Bible.

You love the church, they hate the church.

You love the pastor, they hate the pastor.

Whatever you like, they hate. That's rebellion and it's normal. So during their rebellious stage don't try to teach them anything. There's only one man I know who is dumber than a father who tries to teach a teenager something, and that's a grandfather. It didn't work the first time around, so why are you trying the second time around?

I remember once when one of my sons was about sixteen, I had gone to a neighborhood Bible study. During the Bible study, there was a knock at the door. My son was at the door, really upset and scared.

I asked, "What's the problem?"

He said, "Come outside, I've got to talk to you."

We walked into the yard at our neighbor's house. His voice was trembling as he said he and his friend had been drinking some beer—certainly not a great deal because he obviously wasn't drunk. He just knew I was going to kill him, as he later told me. The friend's father was sitting in his car saying he'd caught them, and he knew they should be severely disciplined. I told my son to go home, and we'd talk about it later. About an hour later, he was in his bedroom. I just told him, "Good night, sleep well, see you in the morning, love you."

He was obviously frightened. But the next morning I said nothing—and never mentioned it again. He later told me that the fact that I didn't pursue it probably meant more to him than anything I ever did in his growing up years. He knew it was wrong. For me to rub it in or make it worse with a judgmental discussion would have been counterproductive. Our relationship was greatly strengthened because I didn't make a big deal of it. I thought if all he had was a little beer, he'd be all right. I wanted to keep a gentle tension between where he was and where I wanted him to be. If I had overreacted and launched into a harsh, judgmental tirade, then I could have lost our relationship and maybe even eventually lost him to drugs and/or alcohol.

None of this is easy.

Grandparents shouldn't try to teach the grandkids a great deal unless they are open and asking for it. They know what you believe simply by watching your actions. Do all your teaching while they're young. Once they become teenagers and rebel, just bless them and pray that God will help them survive until they mature. I don't know why we fathers say things like, "I'm going to teach that boy something even if it kills him."

Those words and the punishment attached to it just kills the parent/child relationship.

We all struggle with this. We all make mistakes. We all have to fight the urge to teach more than we bless, because none of us want to see our children hurt. But our lives, and blessing the lives of our children, speaks louder than any lecture and more powerfully than any punishment. We are better off loving them, explaining things to them, and giving them credit for being able to understand what counts and what is just trivial. One of my grandsons told his mother that he was just certain that I wouldn't come to any of his games because his cousin had football games the same night. I called him on the phone immediately and explained, "Caleb, I want to be sure I come to at least half of your games. I wish I could come to every game, but since your cousin Hunter has games at the very exact same time I can't be both places at once. But I'll be at your games half the time and at his games the other half of the time."

Isn't that better than saying, "Caleb, I can't be in two places at once! Give me a break, I'll get there when I can."

My explanation seemed to satisfy him because he knew I loved him and his cousin because I blessed them both so often.

When my grandson Hunter was ten, he introduced a friend to me.

I gushed, "What a fine young man. I can't decide whether you'd be a great tackle or a guard, whether you should play offense or defense. On second thought, you're too handsome to play defense."

The kid was obviously uncomfortable with my overstatement. Hunter, who is extremely smart, tried to make his friend feel better by saying, "Never mind my papa; he's a preacher, you know, and he talks that way."

I was a little offended that he would dismiss me so flippantly. But then I began to think about it. I changed my mind. What a great compliment that he has been around ministers who talk positively, and that he sees the contrast with his friends at school.

But I also realized that I need to work on my skills with my grandson because Proverbs 22:6 says, "Train up a child in the way he should go, and when he is old he'll not turn from it."

A key is knowing the time, place and way to deliver the blessing. We live in such a negative world that to blatantly inject a blessing into it can sound phony. It must be believable and sincere and given with some understanding of the mind-set and tendencies of the child. It must be delivered in a genuine way. You must earn your right to deliver these hugs, kisses and positive reinforcements.

I don't just bless Hunter with my words, but with my time.

He is extremely interested in archaeology. He loves the pyramids. He is intrigued with the idea of going to Egypt and seeing them. I've often tried to take him there in his imagination and even plan to take him there in reality. To get involved with him in what he is excited about is another way of blessing.

After one of my speeches, a young man came up to me and

said, "You're right."

I asked, "About what?"

He said, "When you said if you have to make a choice between blessing or teaching, always choose blessing."

Why?

"All of my father's family, three generations back, were criminals and went to prison," he said. "My dad was a two-time loser and murderer and spent twenty years in prison. When he finished serving his time, he married my mother, and I was born awhile later. He was a good father to me. I remember him getting into an argument with my grandfather, who wanted my dad to help him with some project. My father said, 'I'm going to spend my time with my son because he's the only thing I've ever done right. I'm going to give myself to this boy because he's a real winner! I don't want to see him go to prison like the rest of us did. He's a great kid and I want him to continue to be one.'"

He stood straight and stuck out his chest and said, "That made me feel so important and so full on the inside. I had a daddy that thought I was terrific. When I heard about a Heavenly Father who loved me and wanted to give me the ultimate blessing, it was easy for me to believe. I trusted Christ—I became a minister. I was able to lead my father to Christ when he was seventy-three. My father was an ex-con, the son of an ex-con and the grandson of an ex-con. He did one important thing right—he blessed me."

Hearing that, I thought of Deuteronomy 30:19: "I have set before you life and death, blessing and cursing . . . choose life."

God said: Choose blessing!

I've been discussing the subtle differences between coaches and dads, but in prison the contrast is stark.

"My dad didn't bless me—he beat me."

"My dad didn't bless me—he raped me."

"My dad didn't bless me—he committed suicide."

"My dad didn't bless me—he ran away."

"My dad didn't bless me—he put me down."

In prison, I see the awful results of an abusive, deserting, addicted, nonblessing father. The contrast is so stark between their dads and mine. I realized quickly what was missing in most convicts' lives—no blessing!

I wasn't a perfect father. My greatest mistake was to sometimes be too positive. By occasionally seeming to ignore or minimize the negatives, my children thought I didn't take their problems seriously. I didn't listen to them long enough; I just started encouraging and blessing. They needed to be heard first. That takes time and patience. My wife never missed much of what was happening at home. She was wise to keep reminding me of my tendency to be so positive. I could come across as unsympathetic to the pain or frustration they were feeling. I can look back over a lifetime of parenting mistakes and successes. I've seen more than thirty-two years of the results of terrible parenting in prison, and I've learned what *not* to do from talking to inmates. You'll never know how well you did until you see the finished product. It happens when you look deep into the faces—and the hearts—of your adult children. I see more of Mavis than myself in them, and I'm very thankful for that. We also had a lot of help with our children from God, family and friends. All three of our children are well-adjusted Christians. They have applied the blessing concept to their own children, and so far, all eight of them are like their parents and grandparents. They are far from perfect, but their development is exciting.

It doesn't matter if you teach a child all the right things or how often you take him to church—how desperately you try to train him morally and spiritually—if you don't bless him, that child will grow up to be a hurting adult. On the other hand, if you fail to train that child as well as you should, but sincerely and consistently bless that child, things will probably turn out all right. Obviously, it would be far better to teach them all the right things and also bless them. But if you can only do one, always favor the blessing.

READER/CUSTOMER CARE SURVEY

We care about your opinions! Please take a moment to fill out our online Reader Survey at **http://survey.hcibooks.com**.

As a **"THANK YOU"** you will receive a **VALUABLE INSTANT COUPON** towards future book purchases as well as a **SPECIAL GIFT** available only online! Or, you may mail this card back to us and we will send you a copy of our exciting catalog with your valuable coupon inside.

(PLEASE PRINT IN ALL CAPS)

First Name		MI.		Last Name

Address				

State		Zip	Email	City

1. Gender
- ☐ Female   ☐ Male

2. Age
- ☐ 8 or younger
- ☐ 9-12   ☐ 13-16
- ☐ 17-20   ☐ 21-30
- ☐ 31+

3. Did you receive this book as a gift?
- ☐ Yes   ☐ No

4. Annual Household Income
- ☐ under $25,000
- ☐ $25,000 - $34,999
- ☐ $35,000 - $49,999
- ☐ $50,000 - $74,999
- ☐ over $75,000

5. What are the ages of the children living in your house?
- ☐ 0 - 14   ☐ 15+

6. Marital Status
- ☐ Single
- ☐ Married
- ☐ Divorced
- ☐ Widowed

7. How did you find out about the book?
(please choose one)
- ☐ Recommendation
- ☐ Store Display
- ☐ Online
- ☐ Catalog/Mailing
- ☐ Interview/Review

8. Where do you usually buy books?
(please choose one)
- ☐ Bookstore
- ☐ Online
- ☐ Book Club/Mail Order
- ☐ Price Club (Sam's Club, Costco's, etc.)
- ☐ Retail Store (Target, Wal-Mart, etc.)

9. What subject do you enjoy reading about the most?
(please choose one)
- ☐ Parenting/Family
- ☐ Relationships
- ☐ Recovery/Addictions
- ☐ Health/Nutrition
- ☐ Christianity
- ☐ Spirituality/Inspiration
- ☐ Business Self-help
- ☐ Women's Issues
- ☐ Sports

10. What attracts you most to a book?
(please choose one)
- ☐ Title
- ☐ Cover Design
- ☐ Author
- ☐ Content

TAPE IN MIDDLE; DO NOT STAPLE

BUSINESS REPLY MAIL
FIRST-CLASS MAIL PERMIT NO 45 DEERFIELD BEACH, FL

POSTAGE WILL BE PAID BY ADDRESSEE

Faith Communications, Inc.
3201 SW 15th Street
Deerfield Beach FL 33442-9875

FOLD HERE

Comments

Personal Application and Prayer

✟ Creative discipline (running on the service road).

✟ Favor blessing over discipline! All true blessers are!

✟ Never discipline in anger. Never attack their self-image while disciplining.

✟ Never go to sleep without getting it straight with all family members. Always make the switch from discipline to blessing. "Do not let the sun go down on your anger" (Eph. 4:26).

✟ Repetition of blessing is seldom overdone.

✟ I love you and bless you just as you are—unconditionally.

✟ Dad had love and respect for the opposite sex, and especially his wife. Our respect for our wives, sisters and mothers is not optional.

✟ Do all your teaching before they get into teen rebellion. There's only one man dumber than a father who tries to teach a teenager something—a grandfather.

✟ If you must choose between blessing and teaching, choose blessing.

✟ God said choose blessing! "I have set before you life and death, blessing and cursing . . . choose life" (Deut. 30:19).

PRAYER

God, help me to teach in a way
my children will listen. Help me to choose
blessing over teaching if I must choose.
God, forgive me for trying to teach
my teenage grandchild.
God, I must be double-dumb.
For Christ's sake, Amen.

Chapter Eleven

SHOW THEM YOUR SCARS

You may think you're too beat-up, too worn down, and too battered and bruised to bless anyone. After what you've been through in your life, who needs your blessing?

Show them your scars.

Stay with me for a moment. Remember that everyone needs a blessing—and that includes you. And you need to bless your family and those close to you—no matter what.

You know what to do. You know about the touch. You know about saying it out loud. You know to tell them they are winners, they are yours and you'll always love them. You know to do it even if it feels strange to you—and them. Most of all you know it works. Your heart tells you that. Your soul tells you that. And yes, God tells all of us that.

Still not sure?

You may think, "Good Lord, what am I doing here?"

Start with, "I'm doing this out of obedience."

When God created us, when we were conceived, God knew the desires of our hearts. He already put in our hearts what he knew would fulfill us. When we obey him, we find contentment. That's the way God gives us the desires of our hearts the second time.

You may say, "Great, I had a father who beat me . . . a mother who ignored me . . . parents who picked at me . . . someone close who abandoned me."

Is that God's way of making me happy?

That's the choices people make . . . to hurt us . . . to leave us . . . to try to steal our hearts. God doesn't take away people's free will. If someone chooses to "go their own way," God doesn't intervene. But he will help pick up the pieces.

Psalm 34:18 reads, "The Lord is close to the brokenhearted. He saves those who are crushed in spirit."

How does that happen?

We show God our scars. We tell him about our wounds. We ask for healing. We accept his forgiveness. We trust that there is a heaven where, as Revelation 21:4 tells us, "God will wipe every tear from their eyes. There will be no more death, or mourning, or crying, or pain. For the old order of things has passed away."

Know how we can begin to dry some of those tears and heal some of those wounds right now—for you and your family?

Bless them . . .

And show them your scars.

Isaiah 53:5 reads, "He was pierced for our transgressions. He was crushed for our iniquities: the punishment that brought our peace was upon Him; and by his wounds we are healed."

We are healed by his wounds. What is the difference between open wounds and scars? Think about that for a minute. The answer is: healing! So many people don't know that. Do you know how many people there are in the world who think they have scars—when what they really have are open wounds? There are even people who have been healed who still think they have open wounds. After Jesus died and God raised him from the dead, do you know the first thing he did when he appeared to the disciples?

He showed them his scars.

John 20:19 says, ". . . Peace be unto you."

Then the Bible tells us, "He showed them His hands, and His side . . ."

Jesus came into the room where the disciples were and wished them peace. Then he showed them his hands and his side—the scars.

Why did he do that?

By showing them his scars just three days after he had been murdered, he was letting them know that God had healed him and raised him from the dead. He did it without a word. He did it by letting them touch, by allowing them to see how he'd suffered. He was blessing them through his scars.

Some of you know that God has healed you, but you are ashamed of your scars. But a scar is proof of healing. Be proud of your scars! Have you ever seen athletes and especially football players show off their scars? They'll say, "This is where I broke my arm . . . this is when I ripped up my knee and the doctors put me back together."

We do this a lot. Sometimes we even compare scars, and that is actually therapeutic because we all have scars. We were all born wounded, and as we grow and live this life, we get more wounds. Jesus showed his scars.

I have a friend named Eddie Siebert. He says he didn't hate his father; he insisted he loved his father. But after hearing me talk about the blessing, he discovered he had some bitterness inside. When you don't get the blessing from one of your parents, you are infected with bitterness.

Eddie told me, "Know why I made straight As in grade school? On one of my report cards in third grade, I got a C, and my mother beat me until the blood ran down my legs, and as I walked away, I left bloody footprints. I was only eight years old. I grew to hate my mother, and it caused a lot of bitterness in me. I didn't even realize it. I thought I had dealt with it. But at my first Weekend of Champions, I stood among the inmates and I knew I had as much or more bitterness than any of them. I realized that love and bitterness cannot occupy the same space. I knew I had to get rid of bitterness. I went forward and accepted Christ when I was a young boy. But I was still hurting. If you've ever met someone who has had a limb amputated, you'll understand what I'm talking about. I have a couple of friends who have amputated limbs, and I asked them if they ever feel the missing foot or arm. They say it's really strange, but in their minds they still feel the missing limb. Sometimes we come to the Lord and he heals us, he amputates all the sin and all the hurt from us—but there is something in us that still feels it. That's bitterness. It's destructive and we need to get rid of it. The bitterness I had toward my mother was affecting my life."

Have you ever met someone who you just absolutely knew was bitter? All of us have. And sometimes they wear the name "Christian," but you can immediately sense a bitter Christian. They're judgmental. They've got a long face. Nothing is ever good enough. They can't be pleased, and they have no joy. What a terrible way to live.

They came to Christ, but they never came to the true healing that God offers. They find it impossible to bless someone else because they don't feel blessed themselves.

That's because they are ashamed of their scars.

Use those scars as reminders of God's healing in your life. Use those scars to show others how God has delivered you from whatever it was that was sucking the life out of your heart and soul. Use those scars so they don't use you. Want to bless someone? First, pray that God shows you if there is any bitterness in your life. Then pray that he shows you how to deal with it. Call that person. Apologize to them. Confront them. Or if that's impossible, meet with a close friend. Talk it out. Pray with that person for deliverance. Accept that friend's blessing. Pour your heart out and show your friend your scars, then watch God come in and heal. It's risky, because it means exposing our true selves to someone else, but God already knows us. And you'd be surprised how a close friend knows you and won't be shocked or condemn you if you open yourself to that person and the Lord.

We often hide our fears. We have skeletons in the closet, that are our unspoken secrets. But if we shine a light into that closet, the ghosts of our fears evaporate. I heard someone say many years ago, "Fear knocked at the door; faith answered and no one was there." Faith always destroys the ghost of fear. Why do I fear? Some traumatic event in my past now shapes my present. Ever watch a horror film? Notice how the demons die in the light? When we tell our secrets, even if only to a trusted friend, they lose their power.

Eddie Siebert said when he confronted his feelings and scars inflicted by his mother, "I got my joy back, and I swore then I would never let anyone, including myself, steal my joy ever again."

Eddie learned that most of the time, it's not someone else who takes your joy—it's you. We steal our own joy. Sometimes we get comfortable with our bitterness.

A man once told me, "I'm just a convict; what difference would it make if I bless my kids?"

I said, "It's even more important that you bless them."

He asked, "Why?"

I said, "Because your kids will think, 'My daddy is in prison, but he doesn't think I'm worth blessing—so I must not be worth very much.' "

The best thing for him to do?

Show his children his scars. Admit that he made mistakes. Admit he knows they feel abandoned because he is in prison. Admit that he could have been a better father.

Then bless them. Tell them that they will always have your unconditional love. Never let them forget they are special and that you will always be proud of them.

The worst thing we can do is let the bitterness and resentment we feel about our own lives poison our relationship with our children.

I remember a defensive end from another team. He would wrap his arms with casts or other hard material and act as if he had an injury and then "use" it to club other players. What a cheap shot! Well, some of us are just like that football player. We don't want healing. We just want to get back at whoever wounded us. We don't want to get rid of our wounds by repenting and asking forgiveness. We just want to wrap our wounds up so people can't touch them, so people don't know where our weaknesses are, and use them to hit others. We don't want to be forgiven for our bitterness because it has become a crutch to justify our own evil attitudes toward others. We also use it to justify the wrong we do. We say, "You know what this guy did to me? I want to do this and it's wrong, but I am justified in doing it because of what he did to me. He hurt me first, and it was worse."

Then do you know what happens? You get to the point where you can't get rid of your bitterness because if you get rid of your bitterness you're left with a load of guilt. Guilt is worse than bitterness. Bitterness steals your joy, but guilt will suck the breath out of your soul and make you miserable. You must get rid of both bitterness and guilt. Let the Lord heal you and set you free. He whom the Lord sets free is free indeed (John 8:36).

Eddie told me, "I'm not ashamed to show my scars anymore. I also found out that I didn't just have scars, I had open wounds. I'm real happy to show you my scars today. I'm not ashamed of my scars. I'm not ashamed to pass on the hope of my salvation and explain the reason for my joy. Jesus showed his scars; I can do the same."

Showing them your scars is helping them, or maybe even healing them. One of the best ways to bless someone is to be honest. Tell them, "I never got a real blessing growing up. I didn't even know that I missed it until lately. Now I realize a blessing is important in everyone's life. I should have blessed you earlier, and I ask your forgiveness. But I intend to do it from now on. I ask that you be patient with me, because this is new and not easy for me . . ."

Then you may get stuck.

Here's a suggestion: Just blurt.

How do you do this?

Rehearse what you want to say. Then blurt! Spit it out fast, so it doesn't freeze in your throat. You don't feel comfortable, you'd rather eat a bowl of worms, but you start talking from the heart. If your scars get in your way, show them your own pain. Tell them that God is still healing you. Don't worry if it sounds stupid or silly, God can take your words and turn them into a message the person will never forget. If Jesus could feed 5,000 with a few loaves of bread and fish, God can take our stumbling speech and send it directly to the heart of someone who needs our blessing.

When my son Billy was sixteen, he was a little rebellious, a little wild. I had recently retired from my pro football career, but I was leading a new and even more exciting ministry of citywide crusades, along with a new and different Weekend of Champions ministry in prisons. I was on the road a lot. It was imperative that I have a good relationship with my family when I was home. I wanted to make the best of my time with them. I was determined to be the blessing father, not the disciplining, demanding, controlling dad. But I overreacted at times. Or I didn't bless him when I should have.

I became an effective "blurter." I would get a running start by saying something like, "I want you to forgive me because I know I was wrong when I yelled at you for scraping the car on the side of the garage."

I was showing him my scars, admitting my temper got in the way and that I wasn't home enough but that I still loved him because he was mine and he'd always be mine. I did that by admitting I was wrong for yelling. I admitted it and asked forgiveness all in one "blurt." I didn't emphasize how he was wrong. I only pointed it out while asking forgiveness for how I was wrong (yelling). If you've been a "blurter" like I was, you can use more of the same with your spouse and your children. It really doesn't matter which way you bless, just make sure you do it.

PERSONAL APPLICATION AND PRAYER

✝ The difference between wounds and scars is healing. Christ showed them his scars, revealing God's healing and resurrection power.

✝ If you have open wounds, there isn't complete healing.

✝ Don't be ashamed to show your scars.

✝ Unhealed wounds can lead to bitterness.

✝ Face your wounds and whoever or whatever caused them, and get it right. Forgiveness is the only way to turn an open wound into a scar. It's also the only way to get your joy back.

✝ When you face your fears and shine the light of confession and faith the fear evaporates.

✝ "Blurting" can be helpful in asking forgiveness.

PRAYER

God, give me the courage to
ask forgiveness of those I have offended.
Make my open wounds into scars,
so that I may be unashamed of your healing.
God, restore my joy that bitterness has robbed.
For Christ's sake, Amen.

Chapter Twelve

CREATIVE BLESSINGS

Years ago, my son Bobby was invited to be the best man at a friend's wedding. He and seven of his former high school football teammates made up the groom's wedding party. They would have been at home in T-shirts and jeans, not tuxedos.

Especially RED tuxedos.

Especially RED tuxedos with PINK shirts.

Especially RED tuxedos with PINK shirts with huge RUFFLES on the lapels.

I arrived before them at the church, and when I saw them get out of a limo and lumber into the foyer, I was tempted to say exactly what I thought, "You girls look really great in those ruffles."

Something else crossed my mind, "You guys look like a bunch of hogs in pink silk shirts!"

Those words nearly came out of my mouth, then I remembered some of my own sermons. I remembered the power of words. I remembered what it was like to be their age and feel self-conscious at weddings, especially when the last thing they wanted to do was wear RED tuxedos with PINK shirts and STUPID ruffles. I remembered they really were doing it to honor their friend on his wedding day.

So I said, "You guys have never looked better. You should wear tuxedos more often."

They stared at me, waiting for the punch line.

"I mean it," I said. "You look sharp."

The more I said it, the more I started to believe it. That's because I saw the hearts inside those red tuxedos and pink shirts. I was glad I had remembered the insecurity of that age, when you are so concerned about what everyone thinks. You act bored, disconnected, but you hear everything. Blessings and curses aren't just spoken, they are bellowed through a megaphone to young men.

They had been walking with their heads down, shoulders stooped, not making eye contact with anyone. After I encouraged them, they began to look up. They seemed to move with more confidence. For the rest of the evening, those young men made a point to come talk to me. Most of the conversations weren't deep, but the idea that they felt comfortable—yes, blessed!—by an older man who is too big to ever look good in any kind of suit was very important. By the end of the evening, a couple of them started to talk about their dreams, their futures, their families. A few words prevented that night from being a nightmare for those guys—and how hard is it to do something like that?

Not very.

But how often do we take the time to help change someone's day?

Teenagers really need encouragement and blessing, even though they act like they don't. They want to appear independent. They are finding their own identity apart from their parents, but they still need to be blessed. When my boys were in their late teens and early twenties and feeling unusually strong, they would sneak up behind me and grab me around the chest and pick me up off the ground. In the process, they were breaking my reading glasses and fountain pens in my pocket.

I told them: "You know the reason you do that? You really want to hug and kiss me, but you don't feel comfortable since you're so big and grown up."

They looked at me strangely.

I said, "I read that the reason older boys want to wrestle around with their dad is because they feel the need for a hug and kiss, but are too embarrassed to do so because they feel it's not masculine."

They didn't react, but I could tell they were listening.

"Since I know now what you really want," I said. "Instead of grabbing me from behind and breaking my glasses and pens, it would be easier to just hug and kiss you! Besides that, you're so strong now you're hurting me."

I have a friend who travels often for his job. He has been married for more than twenty-five years, and his wife always packs his bags and makes sure he gets up and gets out on time to arrive at the airport in time for his flights. Until he came to Christ in 1997, he never said a simple thank-you to his wife for that kindness. He just assumed it would be done for him. Just as he assumed she'd wash his clothes, cook his food and do so many "little things" for him. After his conversion, and after attending several of our Weekend of Champions prison weekends where he heard my blessing speech, he began to bless his wife.

At first, he thought my message to bless was just for parents, and since he didn't have any children, he thought I must have been preaching to someone else. Then he began to really talk to his wife, who also started coming on the prison weekends. As their faith grew together and their communication became more genuine, he realized that he was taking her for granted—that she didn't expect a medal for doing those things for him, but at least he could mention it.

Does thanking a spouse for small favors save a marriage?

Not alone.

Does it help? Does it indicate a sign of love? Does it bless?

You bet.

He tries to remember to thank her when she prepares a special meal, when she changes meal times to fit his schedule, when she helps him with his travel and other commitments. He tells her how they are a great team, a true partnership. He stresses how they are equals, that her role is just as critical as his. He knows she loves to hear the praise, even if she doesn't say much about it. Don't all of us long to be appreciated? To be noticed? Yes, to be blessed?

This letter came from Eddie Siebert:

My good friend Steve Jackson had managed to get me into prison (after two years of cajoling) to help some former football player "minister" to the inmates. I did so to get him off my back and be done with it. When this football guy named Bill Glass got up to share his message, "The Blessing," my immediate reaction was pain from realizing just how much bitterness was inside of me, left over from my own mother's lack of blessing and her life-time of abuse to her children.

Bill never once used the "B" word, but it was painted across my mind in big letters. Bitterness had turned to justification in my mind as I returned ill will for ill deeds, and then that turned to guilt. Incredible guilt hung around my neck like a millstone, along with all the other garbage I was carrying around. I took Bill's advice and got rid of it by forgiving her and cleaning out that room in my heart named "Poor Pitiful Me." "The Blessing" became the best diet that I ever went on because I know I lost about a ton of burden. Intertwined with all of that were my own sons, who I knew I loved more than life itself. My father had blessed me and I thought I was doing a good job with them because:

1. I did not beat my wife.

2. They all had shoes.

3. I had always given them everything they wanted and whatever I had.

4. And yes, I often told them that I loved them.

After hearing "The Blessing," I realized I wasn't doing a lot of things wrong . . . there were some things I wasn't doing right . . . like keeping my love out of reach to bait them to agree with me on moral issues. My unconditional love WOULD BE the basis for their morality.

Finally, I was not telling them at every opportunity that there was nothing they or anyone else could do to change the fact that I loved them, was proud of them, and would always be there for them because they belonged to me . . . and me to them.

About six months later, my sons asked me what prison ministry was doing to me, because I had changed (for the better). I just smiled, hugged them and said, "I love you, I'm proud of you and you are mine."

That was nine years ago and all those close to my family can tell you that we (including my sons) are better and happier people because of "The Blessing" message.

Eddie Siebert kept coming to our prison weekends, becoming more involved in our prison ministry. He is now our CEO and is blessing us back.

It's never too late to bless someone you love.

A very wealthy man heard me talking about the blessing, and afterward he came up and told me, "You know I've got a lot of children and grandchildren, and I don't think any of them care a thing about me. In fact, I think they all pretty well detest me."

I asked him why he thought that was so, and he said, "I guess I keep the blessing just out of reach. I'm always trying to teach them something. I keep telling them if only they had done this or that better."

He called me four different times on the phone and in each case talked to me extensively about how he could bless them. He'd ask, "I grab them by the ears, and what do I say?" He was frightened out of his wits. It was like facing enemy machine-gun fire to talk to his own kids and grandkids and give them a blessing.

Finally, he called them to a hotel in the Caribbean and individually blessed each one of them. He was really frightened about doing this because he had never done it before. I've talked to a few of his grandkids and kids since he did that, and they assured me that it was a great experience they will never forget.

I don't think it's ever too late to give the blessing. I think the children will date time from the day their father was finally able to do it. It would of course be better if it was done earlier, but children and grandchildren need it so badly that they find it a very strengthening experience just to be able to say their dad was finally able to bless them.

When my son Bobby was in his thirties, he told me that he

would never get over the fact that we moved twenty-four times during the first twelve years of his life. I was playing pro football, and half the year we'd live in Texas and half the year we'd live in Detroit or Cleveland—wherever I played pro football. Each time we moved, Bobby had to be taken out of one school and transferred to another. From one set of friends to another. From the North to the South. It must have been a tremendous disruption in his formative years. At first, I tried to pass it off as not being very important. He got right in my face, almost yelling in anger, saying, "I really think you made a big mistake and I resent it."

I quickly saw how important it was to him and said, "I know I was wrong. I'd like you to forgive me. It was selfish of me not to be more sensitive to your feelings. But I will say that I love the way you turned out anyway."

Do you feel guilty because you haven't blessed your children? Maybe you shouldn't get over the guilt, because if you get over the guilt too quickly then you may fall back into the same behavior that caused the problem. The best way to deal with the guilt is to give the blessing. Every time you feel guilty, call them on the phone. Even better, go see them and bless them. Figure out new and better ways to bless them. Be creative. Put as much attention and time into your blessings as you do your job, your favorite hobby or whatever is important to you.

My father was the master of the indirect blessing.

He'd be talking to someone else while I was in the same room, and I'd hear him say, "That boy always amazes me. He is so good-hearted, but he's still rough and tough. I'm proud of him."

My uncle did the same thing, shrewdly allowing me to over-hear him say, "William is very special." My grandfather was even more skilled at indirect blessing. My friend makes a point of praising his wife in front of others—it doesn't matter if she's there or not. He wants it to become a habit, to tell everyone he meets that his wife is terrific, that she's his best friend and that he loves how she's growing in the Lord. It has made their marriage so much better.

There was a time when my young son blessed me. It was in 1966 and I was playing with the Browns. I severely twisted an ankle and had to leave a game early for the first time in twenty years of football at all levels. I was sitting on the trainer's table, feeling discouraged and more than a little sorry for myself. My son Bobby slipped past the policeman at the door, found me in the trainer's room, and with some coaches, players and trainers all standing there, he said, "Daddy, I think you're the best football player in the WHOLE world!"

What more could a father want?

When I talk to my children, my grandchildren, my wife, any of my close loved ones and even some of my close friends, when talking on the phone I'll say, "I better hang up . . . love ya . . . bye."

"Love ya, bye" becomes a little ritualistic, but it is a better way to say good-bye than just to say, "Bye."

I often think if I were to die of a heart attack or stroke, like

I almost did last year, I would much rather be remembered as saying, "Love ya, bye," than just, "Bye."

To ritualize—repeat over and over—an ending to a phone call or to a letter with "Love ya, bye," is not altogether bad—and much better than not expressing it at all. Also, when you do it over and over, it becomes a little bit more natural to do it in more intimate or meaningful ways.

Leave nothing unsaid in the relationship. "I notice you seem sad. Have I hurt you? Have I cheated you in any way? Do I need to ask forgiveness for anything? Could you say at my funeral, if it were to come suddenly and unexpectedly at the end of the day, 'There was nothing between us. There was nothing left unsaid (unconfessed). No roadblocks in our relationship?'" Since none of us are perfect, confession and forgiveness must be a regular occurrence in any good friendship, and the closer the relationship, the more often it will probably occur.

If you want to try it in writing first, that's a good place to start. But rather than just mail a letter, read it out loud. You'll be surprised how even more of your heart will come out as you're reading it, and you may add something to what you've written. When you're finished, you can hand them the letter. Then hug them. I guarantee you, they will treasure that letter and the moment you finally blessed them. Don't stop there. Don't think because you wrote a letter, you're done. A plant needs water every day. We all need food daily. This is a spiritual meal that covers so many of the basic biblical ingredients. Write more letters if you must. There is a place for a written blessing. It's really good to leave blessing notes for your wife or children. My wife often puts notes in my luggage, which blesses me. However, it must not be done in place of, but in addition to, the verbal blessing. Force yourself to look them in the eye. Face-to-face is always best.

Is it ever a bad thing to tell someone you love them, to bless them with your words?

We all know the answer to that.

PERSONAL APPLICATION AND PRAYER

✝ Red tuxedos can be beautiful. Use a blessing to ease insecurity with your children.

✝ Teen boys wrestling with Dad is only a cry to hug and kiss in a masculine way.

✝ Don't take your spouse for granted; she needs blessing also.

✝ Ask forgiveness for child-rearing mistakes. It may help heal open wounds and create healed scars.

✝ Remember the wonderful power of an indirect blessing.

✝ Children blessing parents is the great result and reward of blessing.

✝ Ritual blessings (repeated often) make it easier to find more meaningful and intimate ways to communicate it.

✝ Written blessings can be treasures unless they are substitutes for verbal blessings.

✞ Don't let the sun set on your arguments. Leave nothing unsaid (unconfessed) that would strain the relationship.

PRAYER

God, give me the courage to look into
their eyes and give them an unblinking blessing.
God, give me the right words to say.
For Christ's sake, Amen.

Chapter Thirteen

What We Can Learn from a Blessing

Want to know more about a person?

Find out if they received the blessing.

I'm serious. My biggest mistakes in human relations have always come as a result of ignoring the background of people. In prison, I've come to expect father problems in violent criminals. I'm shocked if it isn't there. When there is no apparent father problem, I always probe more deeply. Sometimes it's purposefully or unintentionally covered up. I know there are exceptions, but it's true at least 90 percent of the time.

How do you know if your marriage will work?

Ask this question, "How do you and your parents get along?"

Ask it during the time you date, and ask it more than once. Watch how the person you date gets along with his/her parents. Listen to how the parents are discussed. Pay close attention. My wife, Mavis, had a fine father who loved her dearly. But he was also raised by a tough father. Mavis's grandmother died when the children were young, and her father had to be both father and mother to his children. He did a good job of rearing them with the help of his older daughters. He was a strict disciplinarian. He had a hard time expressing his love, and he had no idea about the blessing. It was virtually impossible for him to communicate love, so it wasn't surprising that his children struggle with it. Mavis's parents probably did better, considering their background, than could be expected. Both were from single-parent homes.

Mavis's maternal grandfather was killed in a railroad accident when Mavis's mother was two years old. Her grandmother had tuberculosis and couldn't touch her children. She talked to them, but only from across the room. Mavis's mother often wished that she could have just one hug from her mom. Imagine the frustration of mother and daughter in a situation like that. Both want to hug, but they can't. And the child has to be confused. Why doesn't Mom want to touch me? Is there something wrong with me?

Mavis's grandfather was overwhelmed, overworked and feeling underprepared. He struggled to run a store in downtown Calvert, Texas, while raising ten children. Calvert had a population of around 1,000. Half were white and half were black. Main Street was also the highway that went to Bryan and Texas A&M. Papa Knapp ran the General Mercantile Store, selling everything from nails to groceries and even clothes, open twelve hours daily. He was always at the store until after dark. All the boys helped in the store. No hugs and kisses from Dad. Harsh discipline was meted out for even minor offenses. All the boys went to Texas A&M, about fifty miles away. After graduation, they all migrated to the Rio Grande Valley, 400 miles south. It was like Florida, palm trees and citrus fruit, with a warm climate on the Mexican border. The two oldest boys were well established in the automobile business. When the younger three boys graduated from college, they joined their brothers in the business. The older sisters and their husbands were soon a part of the Knapp family business. It was a big, successful and respected family. The children quoted Papa Knapp even after he'd been dead for fifty years. He was honest, hardworking, disciplined and he ran his family like a military school. They fit right in at A&M where everyone was in the military as well as the school. Her dad and his brothers served in World War II as officers and returned to run car dealerships, citrus farms, canning plants and even banks.

Papa Knapp passed on a lot of healthy values and a strong work ethic, but there was also a lack of blessing that continued to show up in the family for generations, as it always does. When Mavis's father first heard me talk about the blessing, he admitted to her, "I don't guess I ever told you that I love you, did I?"

Mavis said, "No, you didn't."

He insisted, "I thought it was just understood!"

She said, "No, I really didn't know you did."

He said, "Why not?"

She said, "It seems to me that if you really loved me, once in fifty years you ought to be able to say it out loud."

He started crying and she did too. They cried for thirty minutes, and of course he was able to say it. I'd never seen him cry before. But once he did, he couldn't help himself. It was a deep, heartaching sob. Mavis cries easily, and she joined in. Pretty soon, I was crying. They cried for a long time, and then he changed. He still had problems with the blessing, and there were many times on the phone even after that when he would call and say, "Your mother and I love you" in a rather stiff tone.

Mavis and I would be on the phone talking to him and I would say, "You mean 'I' love you, don't you?"

And he would say, "Oh yeah, I love you."

It wasn't a natural thing for him—it was a learned thing. But I was so proud of him because it meant so much to Mavis—even if it took some prompting. To her, it was like water on parched earth. It didn't have to be sparkling mountain water coming in a bottle from France. Just real, wet water was enough. She longed for that blessing. It didn't have to sound smooth. It just had to be real, even if he sounded uncomfortable. She loved it. We all have a need for it.

The amazing result is that it did wonders for our marriage. She felt more warmth toward me, and I experienced her love stronger than ever. It shattered some barriers in our relationship. When we were first married, I secretly liked it that she wasn't close to her father. I foolishly thought it would make her more dependent on me. I would be the knight in shining armor saving the damsel in distress. I soon learned that she couldn't be as open and expressive to me because of her father's lack of warmth. The chill is passed from one generation to the next. When she fell into her father's arms and received his blessing, it broke down some barriers in our relationship. Because we were Christians and loved each other, we were able to overcome her father problem.

But in a relationship such as marriage or another important relationship, a key question should be, "How do you and your dad get along?"

In my own marriage, we have worked through these problems and been extremely happy. But the ideal is obviously to not start out behind in the game. Nor is marriage a place to expect a person to make a lot of changes in their personality. Often, the high achievers are the ones whose parents hold the blessing at arm's length—"If only you'd done this, it would have been even better!" Many overachievers are tortured, always striving to prove themselves to an unmoved parent who is cold and distant no matter what. Even if the son or daughter reaches all their goals, the blessing is still withheld. We need to be fathers and mothers, not coaches.

Most families are dysfunctional in some ways, and my family was certainly far from perfect. But the one major thing that both of my parents did right was blessing. Being blessed so strongly by both parents only made me more secure. It was never hard for me to believe in a powerful Heavenly Father who loved me unconditionally.

I simply thought, "You mean God is like my dad and mom and grandparents . . . but much better? Yes, I can go for that!"

So how do you deal with someone close to you who has not been blessed?

You can try to convince that person's parent to do it, as I was able to with Mavis's father. But maybe that can't happen because the parent is dead. Or the parent just refuses.

What should you do?

Remember, any blessing is better than no blessing.

When I first met Mavis, I adored everything about her, even the negative things seemed positive. She was extremely feminine and clumsy. I thought it was cute. I took pride in never being knocked off my feet. I mean just that, knocked off my physical feet! A part of never being knocked off your feet as a defensive end is great balance. She had a hard time with anything that demanded balance. She couldn't ride a bike for constantly crashing. She couldn't go snow skiing without getting hurt. Waterskiing was impossible. Before marriage, it was interesting and attractive. After marriage, it cut into our recreational possibilities. But we worked around it. She was so agreeable and loving. It seemed a minor problem. When we were first married, I liked about 90 percent of the things about Mavis, and not the other 10 percent. As time passed, I discovered the 90 percent of her that I loved overwhelmed the other 10 percent. I just decided to focus on that 90 percent. Now I have to struggle to even remember that annoying 10 percent. When I wrote the above paragraph about what I didn't like, I had to rack my brain to remember what it was. Even in writing it, I was smiling. She's wonderful because she didn't pass on any of her awkward genes to our children. All three have perfect balance. All three have my size—they are large. Well, my daughter, thankfully, is not as big as I am, but is beautiful like her mother—and yet she is a size or two bigger than her 100-pound mother. Fortunately, all three have her good looks and my size and athletic strengths.

For this, I bless her. I say, "What a woman! You passed on all of your strengths to our children."

That's especially true if you use the blessing principle from the beginning of your relationship. Find something to bless your spouse about.

What do you say?

I love you . . . that can never be said enough.

You're a treasure . . . but it must be accompanied with a specific way in which you are great.

You are mine . . . same as blessing a child.

But familiarity makes it even more important to be creative. Variety is just as important as security. Accompany what you say by what you do. Pick out something she hates to do—changing diapers, cleaning bathrooms, cleaning up after the dog—and do it for her. Pick out something she knows you hate to do—and do it for her. Don't demand credit for it or point it out.

Accompany your blessing with flowers, a piece of jewelry, whatever appeals to her. Study her so you know what she genuinely likes and give it to her. But gifts must never be a substitute for verbal blessing. The formula for blessing your wife is a little more sophisticated than for children. It's more like the way you bless your adult children. Believability is most important. But the same three elements must be incorporated: love, value and belonging.

To say, "You are mine," to your wife will only work if you add, "I'm yours."

The "I'm yours" is always weakened by anything that causes jealousy.

Some stupid mistakes that I've made and now avoid: Never admire another woman—even if she encourages you to. Never discuss old girlfriends. If it comes up and must be discussed, point out how much better she is, but even this is dangerous. Also, don't ever try to teach her anything. Love her just as she is! Share feelings and insecurities, which has been very hard for me to do. But don't do anything that would violate her need for security. Many arguments are over money, because money is a symbol of security in most marriages. Handle money carefully. Jesus spoke more about money than he did about heaven and hell. You don't want money to be an obsession, but you do want to make your wife feel secure by taking care of it well, not spending foolishly or selfishly. Remember that life can be like a game of monopoly. After it's over, all the houses and other stuff goes back into the box, and you learn it didn't count nearly as much as you thought during the game. Relationships are what endure, and that's why blessing your wife and children is so important.

So is asking for forgiveness.

When you do, be patient. Wait for an answer.

Ask, "Would you forgive me for raising my voice to you?"

Always name the offense, then let the other person respond. If there is none, repeat the appeal for forgiveness in a new way and again ask, "Will you forgive me?"

Continually search for a chance to show your wife unconditional love. Become a pro at picking out strengths and ignoring weaknesses. And then watch how your wife blesses you back in ways you've never dreamed.

PERSONAL APPLICATION AND PRAYER

✝ Blessing or lack of it predicts behavior. Want a good marriage? Ask how they get along with their parents.

✝ A lack of blessing goes back generations in most families.

✝ Blessings must be said out loud. They are never a given.

✝ How do you and your dad get along? This is a great question to ask in any human relations situation. It even suggests how intimate you are with God.

✝ If God the Heavenly Father is like my dad, except infinitely better, I can go for that.

✝ Concentrate on the things you like about your loved ones and ignore the trivial.

PRAYER

Lord, I thank you for
a blessing father and mother.
They make it so easy for me to bless
my loved ones and even to be closer to you.
For Christ's sake, Amen.

Chapter Fourteen

No Excuses—
Never Give Up!

If you weren't blessed, you can still bless someone else.

And it's never too late.

Always remember—it's never too late for a blessing.

Your life may have been a mess, but you can still bless. You may feel inadequate and disconnected, but you can still bless. You may not even believe it will work, but you can still bless.

Don't think so?

Read this letter from a man named Stephen:

Dear Bill:

The purpose of this letter is to show to you a practical applica-tion of your blessing concept. It took me some time to begin to understand how critical it is to "bless" my daughter rather than attempt to "coach" her to where I wanted her to be. The idea was foreign to me, because I wasn't blessed myself. My father was a good guy, a tough guy, but not the kind who understood why he needed to bless his children, much less how to do it. Something else, I never even heard of this idea until I was in my middle fifties, and believe me, it was very difficult to do at first, but it changed my life.

I was the president of a large biomedical research company that traded on the stock exchange. It was during the mid to late '80s that the AIDS epidemic began to take a foothold in this country. My company developed a promising pharmaceutical, which the National Institutes for Health described as being a significant breakthrough in the treatment of this horrific virus. As you might guess, the stock began to reflect this optimism, which in turn provided my family with a very comfortable lifestyle.

I had four daughters who were the center of my life. In many ways, they were given a higher priority than my wife. My youngest daughter was eight years old and literally went everywhere with me. She was my partner. In 1989, through a number of circumstances, I was indicted for securities law violations. In June 1990, I pled "no contest," on the understanding that I was to be found not guilty by the judge, based on a $2-million-dollar buyout of the securities. When I was unable to acquire the amount of money necessary to make this deal happen, the judge found me guilty of all the charges and sentenced me to 55–83 years in prison.

My wife was devastated. Two of my three oldest daughters were married, with the third daughter in high school. My youngest daughter was only eight, and she owned my heart. Now I went from being with her everywhere to being gone all the time in prison. Within three years my wife wanted a divorce. We were financially devastated. My wife had to go to work and at the same time cope with a little girl who suddenly lost her dad. Not only was her dad gone, she would hear all the comments about her father being in prison.

It was my position that I was innocent of the charges for which I was in prison. To say I was angry was an understatement. It also was my position that we (my family) were Christians and that we had to trust God; we had to be like soldiers. Unfortunately, I became very harsh in this position. Gradually, my wife drifted away. She became tired of hearing my diatribe concerning how she had to live, and how she had to raise my little girl. This led to the divorce.

I used to write strong letters urging my youngest daughter to live completely for Christ. Yes, I always told her I loved her, yet it did not appear unconditional to her. She pulled away from me. She needed to simply know that she was loved no matter what the circumstances were, but I was not able to give her that assurance. I was too busy coaching and pushing her, instead of just loving her.

I spent ten years in prison. When I was released, I had this sense of entitlement. My eight-year-old little girl was now a high school senior. I thought she was obligated to treat me as her dad. She had other ideas, because I wasn't there for her for ten years. I could blame the state and say it wasn't my fault, but I later came to realize that all she knew was that I was gone. She was too young to understand the circumstances.

Meanwhile, my anger was obvious to everyone. I was angry that my wife left me and angry because I'd lost my daughter. For the first year after my release, my daughter would have nothing to do with me. She felt that I was a hypocrite. In 2003, I called her at college and began to accuse her of not standing by me and not treating me like her father—not giving me what I thought I was entitled to. She erupted with tremendous emotion and tears, responding that I didn't care about her. I just wanted someone who didn't exist anymore: her as an eight-year-old.

A friend then told me about your blessing speech, about how we need to bless unconditionally, and do it over and over. I spent too much time pleading my case with her and offering what she considered excuses. I began to tell her that I was sorry for not being there for her—and offered no explanations. I just pled guilty and asked for her forgiveness. I told her that I would always love her, and she could dictate how the relationship should go. The more I thought about the blessing message, the more my heart began to melt. God used that to help me understand that it wasn't my daughter's responsibility to "bless" me; it was my responsibility to "bless" her. I was broken.

She asked me to get to know her as she was now, not to remember her as an eight-year-old. She said we should be just friends. I was challenged by God to begin to love this little girl who had been through so much, who hadn't had a dad. God showed me that I'd been a long-distance coach, and that was destructive to her. God began to do his work in me.

It has taken some time, but I kept blessing her and blessing her and blessing her. Sometimes it didn't seem to be going anywhere, but I stayed with it. And she began to respond. Now she calls me Dad. She asks me for help. She confides in me about what matters to her.

Too often fathers only care about our need to be respected as the head of the house and "the father." I have learned that what I need to do is bring one blessing after another into my child's life. It's through this experience that I began to understand how much God wants to be our father, to have us crawl up on his lap and tell him how much we love him, to give him all our cares and concerns. I have learned that I need to "bless" my children as he has blessed me. I'm not sure that you could say anything more important to fathers than what you have said in your book. With God's strength and help it is my commitment to bless all my daughters and my grandchildren, and not to expect them to bless me.

Still learning to be a father as God has been to me,

Stephen

The key for Stephen was persistence. He knew it felt awkward. He didn't receive an immediate positive response. He wondered if he was on the right track because the idea was new to him. But he was smart enough to know he had nothing to lose. He had already lost his daughter. He had already lost not just ten years, but a piece of his heart and a marriage. He had already lost some so-called friends, millions of dollars and the respected position that he once had in the community. But he wanted his daughter back and was willing to try anything to make it happen. Most of all, Stephen trusted God. He believed God intended him to be a father to his daughter, and he was willing to take an honest look at his own heart and cut through the anger to feel his daughter's pain. He prayed to God to help him bless her, even though he really didn't know exactly what that meant. And God did take over and not only healed that relationship, but two hearts in the process.

He can do the same for you.

Now, are you willing to trust God and do it?

Personal Application and Prayer

✝ Even if you had no blessing, you can still bless. Even if it is not welcomed and appreciated, you can still bless.

✝ Stephen was at the bottom of the heap in prison, but he unconditionally blessed his daughter. Even though she rejected him, he lovingly continued to bless her. She finally gave in and now the relationship is totally restored.

✝ Persistence was the key to Stephen's success. Stephen had lost everything, but he had to understand that she had lost a lot as well. If he was to be a true father, he must meet her needs and forget his.

PRAYER

*Oh God, help me to be a good father
and bless even those who don't bless in return.
For Christ's sake, Amen.*

ABOUT THE AUTHOR

BILL GLASS made a name for himself as one of the most outstanding football players in the National Football League. Giving his life to Christ as a teenager, Bill has been actively engaged in sharing the Gospel of Jesus Christ. While attending Baylor University, he was named an All-American football player, while working with his life-long friend, Dr. Bill Bright, to establish the Campus Crusade for Christ chapter on the Baylor Campus.

Bill was a member of the 1964 Cleveland Browns team that beat the Baltimore Colts to win the NFL World Championship one year prior to the first Super Bowl. During Bill's time with the Browns, he was selected to four NFL Pro Bowl games. "Toughness" was one of the trademarks of the Browns, and Bill Glass played amateur and professional football twenty-two years without missing a game due to injury.

Bill spent the off-season of his pro football career attending Southwestern Theological Seminary. As his football career was drawing to a close, Bill delivered his personal testimony of faith on television during several Billy Graham Crusades. Dr. Graham urged Bill to consider taking on a new career as a full-time evangelist by prompting him to establish his own ministry.

In 1969 Bill founded the Bill Glass Evangelist Association, which today is Champions for Life. After spending all those years playing football in front of thousands, Bill now shares the Good News with thousands of people each year. The highlight of his life has been sharing "The Healing Power of a Father's Blessing" message to thousands upon thousands of men and women each year. This message applies to you whether you are a parent, grandparent, teacher, coach or otherwise work with children. This powerful message can transform their self-esteem and lives of our young people today!

Bill is married to Mavis Irene (Knapp) Glass, and they have three grown children—Billy, Bobby and Mindy. Bill and Mavis enjoy their eight grandchildren and make their home near Dallas, Texas.

You can contact Bill Glass at:

Bill Glass

c/o Champions for Life

P.O. Box 761101

Dallas, TX 75376-1101

972-298-1101

bill@lifechampions.org

For more information on the "The Healing Power of a Father's Blessing," please visit Bill Glass' website at:

www.afathersblessing.com

If you would like to set up a speaking engagement for Bill Glass, please call or write his assistant, Kim Huff, at the above address. Requests can also be faxed to 972-298-1104 or e-mailed to *kim@lifechampions.org*.

Rejoice in faith

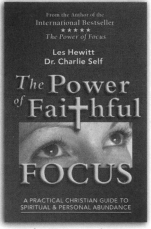

Learn valuable strategies for achieving a healthy and holy balance between the demands of home, church, work and the community.

Code #1185 • $12.95

Based on King David's famous mountain of the Lord passage in Psalm 24, this book offers you a new way of looking at your life of faith and, more importantly, a new and exciting way of living it.

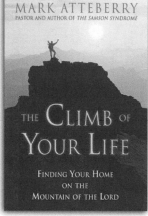

Code #1991 • $12.95

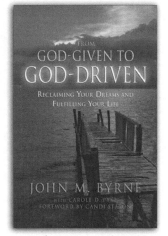

By learning from the teachings of this book, you will not only find happiness and purpose in your life, you will also become a beacon of faith to others.

Code #1746 • $12.95
